First published in 2014 by Motorbooks, an imprint of Quarto Publishing Group USA Inc.,
400 First Avenue North, Suite 400, Minneapolis, MN 55401 USA

Motorbooks titles are also available at discounts in bulk quantity for industrial or sales-promotional
use. For details write to Special Sales Manager at Quarto Publishing Group USA Inc., 400 First
Avenue North, Suite 400, Minneapolis, MN 55401 USA.

To find out more about our books, visit us online at www.motorbooks.com.

ISBN: 978-0-7603-4544-3

Library of Congress Cataloging-in-Publication Data

Falloon, Ian.
  The art of Ducati / by Ian Falloon.
     pages cm
  Summary: "Ian Falloon's The Art of Ducati profiles over 20 historic and contemporary Ducati-brand
motorcycles. The photo sets are accompanied by profiles and tech specs, detailing how and why
these bikes in particular represent the best of the brand"-- Provided by publisher.
  ISBN 978-0-7603-4544-3 (hardback)
  1. Ducati motorcycle. I. Title.
  TL448.D8F3492 2014
  629.227'5--dc23
                              2013049007

Acquisitions Editor: Zack Miller
Design Manager: Cindy Samargia Laun
Cover Design: John Barnett
Design and Layout: Simon Larkin

Printed in China

10 9 8 7 6 5 4 3 2 1

THE ART OF
DUCATI

IAN FALLOON   PHOTOGRAPHY BY JAMES MANN   FOREWORD BY PIERRE TERBLANCHE

CONTENTS

FOREWORD

by Pierre Terblanche

I first met Ian Falloon at the Ducati factory in Bologna some 15 years ago. It is therefore a privilege and great pleasure to have been asked by him to write a foreword for this wonderful new book on the motorcycles of Ducati.

Art indeed.

I grew up in a small town in South Africa called Uitenhage, which is known for its Volkswagen factory and a baboon called Jack, who was formally employed by the South African railways as a signalman. Who, then, could ever have imagined that many years later I would be fortunate enough to end up in Italy as design director for Ducati? During my tenure I was responsible for the creation of many new motorcycles, some of which—such as the 888SPS, Supermono, 999R, MHe900, and PS1000—are featured in *The Art of Ducati*.

The first time that I remember seeing a Ducati was in an issue of *Cycle* magazine (now *Cycle World*) circa 1973. It was love at first sight. When Cook Neilson, against all odds, defeated the best riders in the world to win the Daytona 200 in 1977 on a home built Ducati bevel drive called "Old Blue," I was smitten. Then, a year later, Mike Hailwood won the TT at the Isle of Man on the Steve Wynne 860 and my love turned into obsession. I became a Ducatista.

In those days, Google and the internet were still far-out ideas existing only in the minds of science-fiction writers, so access to information was extremely limited. The highlight of my week was a trip to the Central News Agency to pick up my copies of *MCN* and *Cycle* magazine, my all-time favorite. We lived our motorcycle dreams through the articles and photos in these magazines.

Today it is very different. Many great books are published every year, so we have a huge choice. Ian Falloon's many previous books hold a special place in my collection, but this time he has outdone himself. I have been a designer and student of motorcycles and design for as long as I can remember, and it is always enjoyable and fascinating to rediscover the old favorites in a great new book. The motorcycles selected by the author are wonderful and show that Ian really knows his Ducatis. To top that off, the pictures by photographer James Mann are beautiful.

The "art" aspect of any motorcycle is informed by its design, and the procedures underpinning design have changed radically since the era of the first bike in the book, the 175S, to today's Panigale. In the 1950s and 1960s, design was not a formal process carried out by trained product designers. Instead, passionate craftsmen created the bikes. Wooden models were used to define the shapes of tanks and engine castings. Fairings were crafted by hand-beating aluminum. Frames were fabricated in steel by hand. It was an artisanal approach.

Contemporary designers employ computer-based methods. CAD (computer aided design) is used for engineering and engine design. The bodywork, for example, is the result of a complex procedure beginning with a technical design brief, followed by concept sketches, then clay models, and finally CAS (computer-aided styling) models to create the optical scan information from which the production tooling is created. There's art in the modern approach, but it's not artisanal.

Was it better in the old days, or is it better with precision modern methods? Certainly fit, finish, and quality have improved, but whether a modern water-cooled engine is even remotely close in appeal and beauty to an air-cooled Desmo 750 engine or a 450 single is open for discussion. Let the reader decide.

Pierre Terblanche

The three Ducati brothers (left to right): Adriano, Bruno, and Marcello.

INTRODUCTION

Ducati is one of the most evocative names in motorcycling, its brand synonymous with style, performance, and racing success. Although its history of motorcycle production grew from humble beginnings, Ducati has risen to become Italy's preeminent motorcycle manufacturer. Much of this success was due to the brilliance of engineer Fabio Taglioni, whose legendary desmodromic valve system has been central to Ducati's success on and off the track.

Ducati's story began in 1885 when Antonio Cavalieri Ducati settled in Bologna. Antonio was a renowned engineer, designing and constructing aqueducts throughout Italy, but it was his physicist son Adriano who would inspire the creation of a new electronics company. Adriano pioneered short-wave radio transmission at the same time Bologna-based Guglielmo Marconi was inventing the wireless telegraph. By 1924 Adriano had managed to link Italy and the United States by radio, and in 1926 his father Antonio established the Società Scientifica Radio Brevetti Ducati to leverage Adriano's electronic patents. Adriano was joined by his brothers Bruno and Marcello, and the company prospered. By the mid-1930s the factory in the Bologna suburb of Borgo Panigale (where Ducati still operates today) employed 11,000 people and was the second largest company in Italy.

As World War II roiled, the electromechanical industry was deemed an essential part of Italy's war effort, and here things began to go awry for Ducati. During the early 1940s, production was splintered into several locations, with the German military occupying the Borgo Panigale factory after Italy's withdrawal from the war in September 1943. But the worst was to follow in October 1944 when Allied bombers reduced the plant to rubble.

Italy's postwar scenario was grim. Survival was the goal for most Italian companies, and the Ducati brothers saw the demand for cheap transportation as a path to stability. During 1946 they entered an agreement with auto manufacturer SIATA (Societa Italiana Auto Trasformazioni Accessori, in English, Italian Car Transformation Accessories Company) in Turin to produce the Cucciolo, a 48cc four-stroke single-cylinder engine that attached to a bicycle. Initially produced alongside lenses, radios, and bicycle hubs, the Cucciolo found immediate success, but it still couldn't save the company from bankruptcy. After a couple years teetering on the verge of financial collapse, Ducati finally came under state control in 1949.

The Cucciolo's success saw it evolve into a complete motorcycle, but the plant at Borgo Panigale still labored to service three divisions: mechanics (motorcycles and mopeds), electronics (radios and condensers), and optics (cameras, lenses, and binoculars). Poor management and labor unrest in the early 1950s hobbled the company, but two events guaranteed Ducati's future. In 1953, the mechanical and electrical divisions were separated, and the following year Fabio Taglioni was hired to create a motorcycle capable of winning the important Motogiro d'Italia road race. Taglioni responded with the 98cc Gran Sport, or Marianna, a machine that not only blitzed the Motogiro in 1955, but also established design

By the end of the 1930s, Ducati was one of the largest companies in Italy. The Borgo Panigale factory was bombed heavily during World War II.

criteria for the next generation of racing and production bikes. With a bevel gear–driven single overhead camshaft, the all-alloy unit construction single-cylinder four-stroke soon grew to 125cc and 175cc displacement. By the time production ceased in 1974, the single had gained desmodromic valve actuation and displaced up to 450cc. In racing form, Taglioni's little desmo single very nearly won the 1958 125cc World Championship, and Ducati attracted the attention of U.S. motorcycle distributor Berliner.

The 1960s would prove a difficult decade for Ducati and for motorcycling in Italy in general.

But Berliner's interest ensured Ducati's survival, as the American distributor requested a wide range of models, from scramblers to sporting machines.

The 1970s heralded an era of large-displacement, high-performance motorcycles, and Ducati's new management was enthusiastic to compete in this market. Taglioni responded with another milestone creation, the 750 GT. The GT's 750cc 90-degree L-twin essentially combined two singles on a common crankcase, creating a narrow package that ran smoothly. The 750 had a long wheelbase but set a new standard for stable handling. In the hands of Paul Smart and Bruno Spaggiari, it won the prestigious 1972 Imola 200 race for production-based Formula 750 machines. At this moment the public perception of Ducati changed. Prior to Imola, Ducati was viewed as the builder of quirky and eccentric singles, but Imola proved the company could take on the world's best and beat them soundly. The Imola win inspired the magnificent desmodromic 750 Super Sport and initiated Ducati's practice of producing hand-built race replicas that continues to this day.

By the mid-1970s, economic rationalization resulted in the demise of the venerable overhead camshaft single, as well as the 750 round-case twins. These were replaced by the unloved Giugiaro-designed 860, which, fortunately, evolved into the spectacular 900 Super Sport. When the 38-year-old former world champion Mike Hailwood came out of retirement in 1978 to contest the Formula 1 race at the Isle of Man, he chose a 900 SS-based NCR racer. His resulting win on the island inspired Ducati's most successful model of the early 1980s, the Mike Hailwood Replica. The bevel-drive engine was on life support by this stage, however. An all-new engine was in the wings, powering the mid-displacement Pantah. The new engine's economical and simple toothed rubber belts replaced the expensive and complex bevel gears of the old twin.

The Pantah grew to 750cc, powering Tony Rutter to four TT2 World Championships. Behind the scenes, though, Ducati was under government control and the future of motorcycle production looked bleak. Fortunately, the Castiglioni brothers—owners of Italy's Cagiva motorcycle company—were able to purchase Ducati in 1986, thus ensuring the company's next critical development, the Desmoquattro powerplant. The new engine was an evolution of the Pantah, but it was reworked extensively to include four-valve desmodromic cylinder heads, water-cooling, and electronic fuel injection. It was the beginning of a new, and highly successful, era.

Ducati began producing high quality half-frame micro cameras in 1941.

The Desmoquattro initially displaced 851cc but soon grew to 888cc and then further evolved into Massimo Tamburini's iconic 916 in 1994. By the time the Desmoquattro finished in production in 2002, it was displacing 996cc and had garnered multiple World Superbike Championships, primarily in the hands of British rider Carl Fogarty.

Ducati's next major evolution was the Testastretta-powered (narrowhead), Pierre Terblanche–designed 998 and 999, which eventually begat the 1098 and 1198. Ducati's lineup expanded significantly during the Desmoquattro and Testastretta eras with offerings as diverse as the highly successful Monster, ST sport tourer, Multistrada adventure bike, Hypermotard, and limited-edition retro models such as the Mike Hailwood 900e and Paul Smart 1000.

Flush with success, Ducati entered the highest level of motorcycle competition, MotoGP, in 2003. This culminated with Casey Stoner winning the 2007 World Championship and the release of the first (and only) production version of a MotoGP bike, the 2008 D16 RR.

As Ducati moves forward under Audi ownership, new models challenge traditional Ducati concepts. The 2011 Diavel redefined the cruiser class, and the Superquadro engine powering the Panigale is a clean-sheet, revolutionary design.

Despite technological revolution, Taglioni's desmodromic 90-degree L-twin configuration continues to beat at the heart of every Ducati. No other motorcycle manufacturer has so gracefully merged design and technology for so many decades. And therein lies *The Art of the Ducati Motorcycle*.

The legendary engineer Fabio Taglioni set Ducati on its path to greatness.

PART I

SINGLES

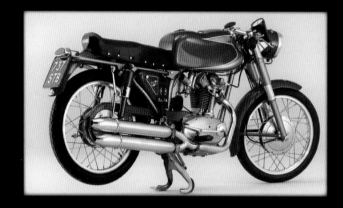

CHAPTER 1

175 SPORT

(Silverstone) 1960 | 175cc air-cooled OHC single | 62mm bore | 57.8mm stroke | 14hp at 8,000rpm | 230lb (104kg) | 81mph (130kmh)

Every time a Ducati wins a race, it continues a tradition begun in 1955 with the single overhead camshaft Gran Sport, or Marianna. The Gran Sport was the first Ducati designed and built with racing in mind, and its success ensured that racing would become a predominant feature in the company's history. Before the Gran Sport, Ducati's racing machines were based on the 48cc Cucciolo. When Gran Fondo road races such as the Milano-Taranto and Motogiro d'Italia were resurrected, Ducati hoped for success with its new overhead-valve 60 Sport.

Taglioni's Gran Sport, or Marianna, was Ducati's first successful racing design. This engine formed the basis for the production 175.

The Motogiro d'Italia was a nine-day stage race run on normal Italian roads and limited to motorcycles displacing less than 175cc. In the 1953 and 1954 Motogiro, Ducati was completely outclassed by Laverda. Because success in the Gran Fondo races was considered pivotal for sales, Ducati's managing director Dott. Giuseppe Montano hired engineer Fabio Taglioni away from Mondial to design a completely new motorcycle. Only one month after the 1954 Motogiro defeats, Taglioni began work on the Gran Sport, and Ducati's illustrious competition story was underway.

Taglioni always worked with surprising speed, and he showed a remarkable ability to get designs right the first time. Few designs exemplified this better than the Gran Sport, later nicknamed the Marianna. Its advanced engine design was conceived for racing first and production second, thus it proved virtually unbeatable in Italian road races. So forward-thinking was the Marianna's design that it would form the basis of the Grand Prix desmodromic racers and a range of racing and production machines through 1974. In fact many of its design criteria carried through to the later 90-degree V-twins, and even the current Testastretta and Desmodue owe much to the Marianna. This was truly one of Ducati's great engine designs.

The hand-built, limited-production Marianna bore little resemblance to the mundane overhead-valve singles Ducati was producing during 1955 and 1956. Taglioni realized that there was no point in having a successful racer without a comparable production version. Ducati rectified this in 1957, initially with the 175 Sport followed soon afterward by the 175 T (touring). These were the first series-production motorcycles to bear Taglioni's stamp, and the 175 Sport set a reputation-making trend that continues to this day: Ducati's production adaptations of its successful racers.

The 175 Sport was the first production bevel-drive single, but it soon begat a range of singles eventually encompassing displacements from 100cc to 450cc. The heart of the little engine was a set of vertically split die-cast

aluminum-alloy crankcases, with a tower shaft and two sets of bevel gears driving a single overhead camshaft. The design was quite advanced for the day, with a wet sump, unit-construction four-speed gearbox, and primary drive by helical gears. The two overhead valves were set at a wide 80-degree included angle, an arguably obsolete approach that required a very high-domed piston to obtain a high compression ratio and compromised combustion efficiency. This cylinder head design was arguably obsolete even in 1957, but it would last nearly 30 years, all the way through Ducati's final bevel-drive twin, the Mille. Hairpin springs closed the valves, but unlike the Marianna these were enclosed to keep the engine oil tight. Another trademark feature that would carry though for nearly 30 years was a pressed-together crankshaft riding in ball bearings. This carried a one-piece connecting rod with a bushed small end and a roller-bearing big end. A single 22.5-millimeter remote-float bowl Dell'Orto carburetor handled breathing, and the fuel/air mixture was squeezed at a very mild 8.0:1 compression ratio. The handsome all-alloy engine looked like exactly what it was: a race-bred engine adapted for the street.

Other 175 Sport features would also become Ducati trademarks. The single downtube frame used the engine as a stressed member, and the chassis was suspended by basic telescopic forks and twin rear shock absorbers. Though the full-width drum brakes were large for such a small motorcycle (180 millimeters on the front and 160 millimeters on the rear), the 18-inch tires were narrow (2.50 and 2.75 inches). Typically Italian features included a weak six-volt electrical system and marginal lighting.

The Marianna dominated the Motogiro d'Italia beginning in 1955. This is Franco Farnè in the final 1957 event.

A number of unique components distinguished the early 175s, including a rubber-bushed single front-engine mount and a bolt-on rear-frame loop. Later production versions showed greater uniformity of components.

The 175 Sport's design also set it apart from other motorcycles in 1957, particularly its unique fuel tank. Though lovely in its execution, it was designed purely to follow function with arm recesses sculpted into the tank to allow a crouched rider to hug the motorcycle while gripping the clip-on handlebars. There were even eyelets atop the tank to secure a chin pad for those boy racers who really wanted to get their head down.

By modern standards, the 175 Sport is a tiny motorcycle. The wheelbase is a short 52 inches (1,320 millimeters) and the seat height only 31 inches (790 millimeters). The rider needed to be jockey-sized and stuck to the tank like a decal to obtain the claimed maximum speed of 80 miles per hour. When the 175 Sport debuted at the Milan Motorcycle Show at the end of 1956, it was a sensation. The garish color scheme and racing orientation was unprecedented from Ducati, a company known for Cucciolos and unexciting pushrod singles. Here was a bold statement that Ducati was serious about building sporting motorcycles based on their successful racers.

So successful was the 175 Sport that it caught the attention of American motorcycle importer Berliner, who saw a future for these little singles. Ducati responded to the American market with the Scrambler and Americano. The 175 Sport continued for some time after the introduction in 1958 of the 200. In the United Kingdom, the 175 was sold as the Silverstone and Silverstone Super through through 1961. Ducati was on the world map. Today the 175 Sport may seem generations removed from a Desmosedici or Panigale, but this was ground zero for Ducati's legend.

In response to US importer Berliner's request, the 175 grew to 200cc for 1959.

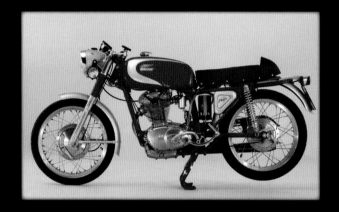

CHAPTER 2

250 MACH 1

1965 | 248cc air-cooled OHC single | 74mm bore | 57.8mm stroke | 27.6hp at 8,500rpm | 256lb (116kg) | 106mph (170kmh)

After a decade of buoyant sales and racing success, all Italian motorcycle manufacturers faced difficulties during the 1960s. The advent of affordable cars virtually destroyed the market for basic motorcycle transportation throughout Europe, though Ducati was shielded from much of the economic downturn thanks to its government ownership. Many Italian motorcycle companies simply closed their doors during this period.

Ducati, like many manufacturers, saw its future in the U.S. market. But success in North America would require larger displacement motorcycles. Ducati's 175 had grown to 200cc largely at Berliner's behest, and during 1961 it released the 250 F3 production racer. This limited-edition machine was extremely expensive, but a production 250 street version soon followed. This new "narrow-case" 250 would form the basis of the overhead camshaft production range until the "wide-case" singles of 1968 debuted. The 250 was initially available in two versions: the touring Monz a and the more sporting Diana. The Diana was a true café racer with clip-on handlebars and had a claimed 24 horsepower. A race kit was also available, featuring a 9:1 forged piston, Dell'Orto 27-millimeter SS1 remote float-bowl carburetor, and a megaphone exhaust. American club racers preferred to modify their machines and adopted the Diana enthusiastically, often in preference to the exclusive 250 F3.

In mid-1963 Ducati released its ultimate four-speed production bike, the 250 Mark 3. This 30-horsepower modified Diana was a serious production racer. Full racing equipment included clip-on handlebars; minimalist, race-regulation fenders; performance tires; and a competition number plate. It looked brilliant in its blue and silver gas tank with matching blue frame. In April 1964, the Mark 3 was upgraded with a five-speed gearbox. This version would evolve into one of Ducati's all-time classics, the 250 Mach 1.

Impetus for the Mach 1's release came from the success of Bruno Spaggiari and Giuseppe Mandolini on a 284cc prototype racer in the 1964 Barcelona 24-hour race at Montjuich Park. A tight racing budget in the early 1960s meant Ducati's factory-backed race wins were rare and sporadic. To encourage privateer involvement, Ducati produced the limited-edition Mach 1/S production racer. This racer didn't achieve the results expected, but its street derivative, the Mach 1, was the bike that many Ducati enthusiasts had been waiting for.

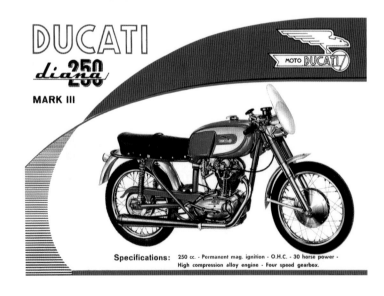

The US-only 1963 250 Mark 3 was the forerunner to the Mach 1.

After the introduction of the Mach 1 (right), the Mark 3 (left) gained high handlebars but retained rear-set footpegs.

Ostensibly the Mach 1 engine was the same as that in the Mark 3, but more highly tuned. It retained the 10:1 compression ratio and unfiltered Dell'Orto SS1 29D carburetor, but it had larger hairpin-type valves (40-millimeter exhaust and 36-millimeter intake) and a hotter gray-coded camshaft. Unlike the U.S.-spec Mark 3, the Mach 1 had battery and coil ignition. A rear-set rocking gear change pedal operated the five-speed gearbox. Clip-on handlebars were standard, but there was also the bizarre option of a Mach 1 with rear-set foot controls and high, touring-style handlebars.

Despite the increase in alternator output to 60 watts (from 40 watts), the electrics remained weak, with the six-volt 25W headlight providing illumination little better than that of a candle. But customers didn't buy the Mach 1 for its night-touring abilities. Mach 1s sold because they had all the right ingredients for a top 250cc sporting street bike. With a quality Marzocchi suspension in front and rear, minimal weight, and a short 1,350-millimeter wheelbase, the Mach 1 could more than hold its own in the handling department and provided an exquisite balance between power and weight. Full-width drum brakes hauled the little sport bike down in quick order.

While much of the chassis and rolling stock was the same as the other 250cc Ducati singles, the Mach 1 was the only version with a red frame and a wildly optimistic 150 miles-per-hour (240 km/h) Veglia speedometer. Ducati claimed the Mach 1 was the world's fastest 250, and although this claim was optimistic, the Mach 1 was still the sporting 250 to have in 1965.

The Mach 1 wasn't widely available in the United States, so the 250 Mark 3 continued as Ducati's top performance model in 1965. But for 1965 the Mark 3 specification was updated, making it similar to the Mach 1, albeit with a black frame, high handlebars, and magneto ignition. The factory claimed a higher top speed of 110 miles per hour (177 km/h) for the Mark 3 and accentuated its sporting nature with a supplementary 100-millimeter Veglia tachometer and a racing plate over the headlight. The claimed weight for the 1965 Mark 3 was also slightly less than the Mach 1 at 247 pounds (112 kilograms).

The Mach 1 continued through 1966, as did the Mark 3, but the lattter was no longer the café racer it had once been. Mach 1 production finished after 1966, though the Mark 3 continued. However, even with the new wide-case replacement imminent, the Mach 1 (and narrow-case Mark 3) continued to be the favored choice amongst privateer racers. In 1969, Alistair Rogers gave Ducati its first TT victory in the 250 production race at the Isle of Man. His Mach 1 racer turned an average speed of 83.79 miles per hour (134.84 km/h).

The 250 Mach 1 exemplified the finest characteristics of the narrow-case Ducati single. It had everything a classic Ducati required: performance, looks, and balance. One of Ducati's most outstanding production bikes of the 1960s, the Mach 1 has earned its cult status.

CHAPTER 3

350 MARK 3 DESMO

1968 | 340cc air-cooled OHC single | 76mm bore | 75mm stroke | 30hp at 8,000rpm | 282lb (128kg) | 103mph (165kmh)

The mid-1950s was a golden age for Grand Prix motorcycle racing, and competition in the 125 category was fierce. Fabio Taglioni dreamed of winning a World Championship with his new 125cc overhead camshaft single, but he knew it needed more power. Only a year after the Marianna's debut, Ducati unveiled the Bialbero, a double overhead camshaft version. Ostensibly a Marianna with a new cylinder head, the Bialbero was raced during 1956 with little success. The Bialbero's reliability was dubious at sustained high revs, due to problems with valve float and minimal valve-to-piston clearance. There was no room for error if the rider missed a gear.

Taglioni's solution was to eliminate valve springs entirely with a method of positive valve control known as desmodromic valve actuation. The desmodromic idea wasn't new. Taglioni had already designed engines employing a desmodromic valve layout, and Mercedes had been successful in 1954 and 1955 with its desmodromic Grand Prix and sports cars. Taglioni's solution involved a replacement cylinder head for the Bialbero, with gear-driven triple camshafts—the opening camshafts sitting over the valves and the closing cams mounted on a single central camshaft, operating the valves with forked rockers.

Taglioni's desmo 125 won its debut race, the nonchampionship 1956 Swedish Grand Prix, and after a year of development it was ready for a full assault on the 1958 125cc World Championship. The desmo Ducati won three of the seven races that year, with Alberto Gandossi just failing to beat Carlo Ubbiali's MV Agusta for the title. It was close, but not close enough, and after 1959 Ducati management decided to quit factory racing. Ducati pensioned its little desmo racers. Taglioni had to wait nearly a decade for his dream of building the first production motorcycle engine with desmodromic valves to become reality.

In 1968 the updated wide-crankcase single replaced the narrow-crankcase type. This new design alleviated some of the earlier design's weaknesses and allowed for a capacity increase up to 436cc. The selector box internals were improved, the gear cluster updated, and the main bearings enlarged. Oil sump capacity increased to 2.5 liters, and the crankpin was larger. The wider rear engine mounts and a twin downtube rear frame section strengthened the frame. The new frame made possible a host of further improvements, including a revised swingarm and a sturdier center stand. An updated electrical system was another key improvement. A new alternator and regulator powered a revised headlight that included an ignition switch mounted under the headlight shell that didn't allow water to enter. Still, many components were carried over, notably the suspension, brakes, and 18-inch wheels.

Paul Smart was a successful Ducati rider long before his famed Imola win. Here he is on his way to victory at Brands Hatch on a desmo single in 1968.

The 1968 Mark 3 was similar to the desmo but finished in red with a red frame.

During 1968, the wide crankcase engine went into production, initially as the 250 and 350 Scrambler, followed shortly afterward by the 250 and 350 Mark 3 and Monza. The 250 Mark 3 engine was in Mach 1 tune, and the 350 Mark 3 featured the more highly tuned engine of the 350 Scrambler, but due to the bike's weight increase, the performance wasn't as strong as the earlier versions. The Mark 3's distinctive styling included a twin filler-cap gas tank, inherited from the unusual 1967 two-stroke 50 SL/1. This unique feature would appear only on 1968 models. What the Mark 3 really needed was Taglioni's engineering tour-de-force: the desmodromic cylinder head.

Unlike the triple camshaft 125 Grand Prix Desmos, the production desmo retained a single overhead camshaft, incorporating both opening and closing lobes with hairpin valve springs retained to assist in starting. The springs assisted starting by seating the valves the final few thousands of an inch so that there was no loss in compression as the engine turned over. The springs were the same as those used with the 160 Monza Junior, but they were still considerably stronger than the small closing springs fitted to the later desmo twins. The desmodromic cylinder head was all new, including new castings, rockers, valve guides, collets, rocker shafts, and bushes. The cam end cover proudly proclaimed "Desmo."

Though Ducati wasn't officially involved in racing, Taglioni did manage to produce a prototype single overhead camshaft racing desmo single. Franco Farnè debuted this desmodromic 250 at Modena early in 1966, and in 1967 a prototype 350cc wide-crankcase desmo engine was developed. Gilberto Parlotti and Roberto Gallina campaigned this prototype engine with moderate success in Italian street-circuit events. Bruno Spaggiari headed the rider lineup for 1969, providing an encouraging fifth place in the Italian 350 Grand Prix at Imola behind the Yamaha and Jawa two-strokes.

Back on the street, there was very little to differentiate the desmo version from the standard Mark 3. The Desmo was finished in slightly less-flamboyant colors (a black rather than red frame and a cherry-red tank rather than Italian racing red), had a chrome-plated headlight and fenders, and had a small "D" decal on the side panels. Apart from the cylinder head, the engines were identical, and there really wasn't much of a performance differential between the two models in standard trim. The desmo engine was fitted to the 250 and 350 Mark 3, creating two new models: the 250 Mark 3 Desmo and the 350 Mark 3 Desmo. When fitted with a megaphone exhaust, the 350D claimed a top speed of 112 miles per hour (180 km/h), making it the fastest production Ducati single ever offered. Each Desmo was provided with a test certificate, and all any boy-racer needed were rear-set footpegs to go with the clip-on handlebars.

Several options were available for the Desmo, including a high, touring style handlebar and a race kit. This kit contained a race camshaft, a range of main jets, a megaphone, and a full fairing. The early Desmos were successful privateer race bikes, with one winning a 1970 250 Production TT race at the Isle of Man (Charles Mortimer aboard the Vic Camp Mark 3 Desmo).

With their twin filler tanks, Dell'Orto SS1 carburetor, and auxiliary white-faced Veglia tachometer, the 1968 Desmos were superb sporting motorcycles. They also established the Ducati desmodromic tradition that continues to this day.

CHAPTER 4

450 SCRAMBLER

(Jupiter) 1971 | 436cc air-cooled OHC single | 86mm bore | 75mm stroke | 23hp at 6,500rpm | 282lb (128kg) | 81mph (130kmh)

Yamaha's DT-1 of 1968 is credited with establishing the on/off-road dual-purpose trail bike, but Ducati had begun producing motorcycles of this genre more than a decade earlier. Ducati's initial foray into the off-road world was in 1958 with the 175 Motocross. This serious off-road machine featured a special frame, suspension, brakes, and tuned engine. The 175 soon became a 200, but no one in the late-1950s off-road racing world had heard of Ducati, so these early Motocross bikes failed to find success.

When the single grew to 250, Berliner in the United States requested a new machine suitable for street riding, road racing, short-track racing, and scrambles. It was a tall order, but in 1962 the 250 Scrambler appeared. Unlike the Motocross, the Scrambler featured mostly standard production components, notably the frame, brakes, and forks. By 1966, the Scrambler had lost its off-road pretensions, along with its motocross tires and quick-detach lighting. Basically, Scramblers were stock roadster Mark 3s with dual-purpose styling, thus making them among the first motorcycles to emphasize form over function. They were highly successful, particularly in the United States and Italy, and continue to enjoy cult status in Italy.

When the new wide crankcase engine appeared in early 1968, it was initially installed in the 350cc Scrambler and the 350 Sport Scrambler in the United States. The stronger, more reliable wide crankcase engine design also allowed for an increase in capacity beyond 350cc. The 450 (actually 435.7cc) was released in 1969 and featured a new crankcase, cylinder, cylinder head casting, and crankshaft. Ducati was unable to create a full 500 because the 75-millimeter stroke was the longest that the crankshaft throw could accommodate without smacking the gearbox pinions. A larger engine displacement would have required redesign and retooling. All 350 and 450 Scramblers for 1969 received the new square-slide 29-millimeter Dell'Orto VHB carburetor. The carburetor inhaled through a new air filter, and the engine exhaled through a shortened Silentium silencer.

A number of other key changes were incorporated with the introduction of the 450 Scrambler. The frame was braced with additional gusseting along the top tube underneath the gas tank, and the final drive included wider sprockets and a larger drive chain. All 1969 Scramblers received chromed gas tank side panels and a slightly longer Marzocchi front fork.

Updates for 1970 were minor and included locating the instruments (now CEV) in individual housings and revising the 450's crankpin to a 30-millimeter diameter. Scramblers retained this configuration until 1973, when they became very similar to the range of Mark 3 roadsters. These final Scramblers were even less off-road oriented than the first wide crankcase versions, with street Borrani wheels, road brakes, and a Marzocchi fork without protective gaiters.

The original 450 Scrambler evolved into the 450 R/T, one of the more interesting bikes to emerge from Borgo Panigale during this period. Like the original Scrambler, the R/T was created at the request of Berliner, which was seeking a dual-purpose bike with more off-road capability. Compared to the Scrambler, the R/T was a much more serious off-road bike. R/T stood for "Road and Track," and its off-road abilities easily matched those of Yamaha's popular DT and Honda's SL. In fact, R/T could have been interpreted as "Race and Trail," "Rorty Thumper," or even "Revenge on Two-Strokes."

The silver-painted R/T frame and cycle parts were unlike those on any other production Ducati. The frame borrowed from the twin-cylinder 750 GT,

The 450 R/T was a more serious off-road motorcycle than the Scrambler.

Ducati was rather optimistic in promoting the 450 Scrambler as a true off-road motorcycle.

featuring its tapered-roller steering head bearings. With its 21-inch front and 18-inch wheels mounted with Pirelli Cross tires, and a tiny 160-millimeter front brake from the 160 Monza Junior, the R/T was aimed squarely at the off-road market. Additional off-road specification included a sump guard, chain guide, chain oiler, snail-cam chain adjusters, quick-detach lighting, and racing plates. The Marzocchi suspension was designed specifically for the R/T. Its 35-millimeter fork featured dual oil seals and 7 inches of travel, while the rear shock absorbers were 320 millimeters long.

Ultimately the R/T proved too heavy to function as a serious dirt bike, and it was less popular than was expected. Production ran barely a year. Perhaps its greatest glory came in 1971, when Ducati provided a complete lineup of seven R/Ts for the Italian Trophy Team to campaign in the International Six-Day Trial. Though these factory bikes looked promising, they were no match for the light and quick CZ and Jawa two-strokes.

The less sharply focused Scrambler, on the other hand, had no promises to fulfill. It was never really intended as a true dual-purpose motorcycle with off-road capability, despite Ducati's somewhat optimistic advertising. Instead, it was a capable all-rounder, and in that role the Scrambler hit the bull's eye. Its success saved the company from extinction in the early 1970s.

CHAPTER 5

450 DESMO

1974 | 436cc air-cooled OHC single | 86mm bore | 75mm stroke | 27hp at 6,700rpm | 280lb (127kg) | 99mph (160kmh)

When Ducati first released the 450 overhead camshaft single, it was intended to power the Scrambler. But Taglioni saw a performance future for the 450, so a desmodromic street version was offered beginning in 1969. The original version was styled similarly to the 250 and 350 Mark 3 Desmo. At the same time, Taglioni was developing a 450 racing version for Bruno Spaggiari to ride in the 1970 Italian Championship. The competition version was derived from the production 450 Desmo, but it was enhanced with a twin-plug ignition, larger valves, a 42-millimeter Dell'Orto carburetor, and a 10:1 compression ratio. These modifications produced 50 horsepower at the rear wheel. The racer also had a reinforced swingarm and a 210-millimeter Fontana front brake; it weighed only 264 pounds (120 kilograms). The results were encouraging, but the desmo single was no match for the multicylinder MVs, Benellis, Lintos, and Patons. Development ceased, and Taglioni turned his attention to creating a 500cc V-twin.

With the competition version of the 450 Desmo shelved, Ducati decided to update the style and create a superior sporting machine. While the 450 Desmo engine was unchanged from earlier production versions, the same couldn't be said for the appearance or running gear. Earlier desmo singles had retained the old-fashioned 31.5-millimeter Marzocchi enclosed fork and Grimeca single-leading shoe brakes, basically identical to the original overhead camshaft 175 of the late 1950s. The 1971 Desmo singles set aside the antiquated suspension and brakes and featured a sturdier 35-millimeter Marzocchi fork with comparably stronger rear shock absorbers. The front brake was uprated to a much more powerful double-sided unit, and lightweight Borrani 18-inch aluminum wheels rims replaced the steel type.

What really set the 1971 Desmo singles apart from the earlier machines, however, was their metal-flake silver fiberglass bodywork complemented by an abbreviated front fender and racing-type solo seat. Clip-on handlebars, rear-set footpegs, and an instrument layout dominated by a large 85-millimeter white-face Veglia tachometer further accentuated the Desmo's sporting intentions. Really, only the barest concessions were made for street legality. The silver desmo singles continued for 1972, but they were about to receive their final update.

During 1972 Ducati was in limbo as it awaited the completion of a new factory expansion dedicated to production of the new 750 twin. While Ducati upgraded its factory, Leopoldo Tartarini of nearby Italjet began the task of restyling the desmo singles. Tartarini had a long association with Ducati, riding a factory Marianna in the 1955 Motogiro d'Italia and a prototype 175 dual overhead cam twin in the 1957 race. Following the cancellation of other 1957 road events, and still under contract to Ducati, Tartarini, with his friend Giorgio Monetti, embarked on a yearlong "round the world" publicity trip on a pair of new Ducati 175s. On his return, Tartarini established his own motorcycle business, Italjet, and during the 1960s produced a range of motorcycles on proprietary platforms. These included the Grifon, based on the Triumph 650, and the Indian Velocette and Royal Enfield Interceptor for Floyd Clymer in the United States.

Tartarini made minimal changes to the silver desmo singles, but he created a completely fresh look for 1973. Central to his redesign was a bright yellow color scheme, accented by black stripes. This color scheme would be echoed in the 1973 750 Sport. The gas tank was now steel instead of fiberglass, and the solo seat incorporated the rear fender and a rectangular taillight. The desmodromic engine was largely unchanged, still available as a 250, 350, or 450, but now adopted a Ducati Elettrotecnica electronic ignition. Although the ignition was innovative, and undoubtedly improved starting, the remainder of the six-volt electrical system was a relic of the 1960s. The weak 80-watt alternator managed barely enough juice to charge the battery with the headlight on.

The updated 1973 Desmo single retained the 35-millimeter Marzocchi fork, Borrani 18-inch wheels, and double-sided Grimeca drum brake. New features included a pair of small instruments in pods attached to the top triple clamp and a 150-millimeter Aprilia headlight. The hand and rear-set foot controls carried over from the previous silver version.

Ducati sponsored Spaggiari's racing school with 450 singles during 1970. Fabio Taglioni is in the center.

The desmo single received its final updates in 1974, with the most significant changes made to the front brakes and suspension. A 280-millimeter cast-iron disc and twin-piston Brembo brake caliper and master cylinder, similar to those on the 1974 750 GT and Sport, replaced the Grimeca drum. This single disc arrangement always felt underpowered and taxed on the 750, but it suited the desmo single perfectly. A 35-millimeter Ceriani fork replaced the 35-millimeter Marzocchi unit.

With its electronic ignition and front disc brake, the final desmo single was something of an enigma. In many respects, the single was still a remnant of the 1950s. The single downtube frame, hairpin valve springs, and six-volt electrical system all harked back to an earlier era. Its overall dimensions were also indicative of an earlier age. Compared to Japanese 450 twins of the day, the yellow desmo was lighter, shorter, and much more compact. But the 450 Desmo was still a single. Vibration was prevalent, and it was no powerhouse. Still, get one on a smooth, twisty road and it is one of the most satisfying vintage sports motorcycles. Compared to the long, heavy-steering bevel twins, a desmo single is light, short, and agile.

The desmo singles were always expensive to manufacture, and production ceased after 1974. They were pure machines—nothing unnecessary in the specification and no concession made to civility, noise, or emission controls. This was motorcycling minimalism, and the 450 Desmo single represented the end of an era.

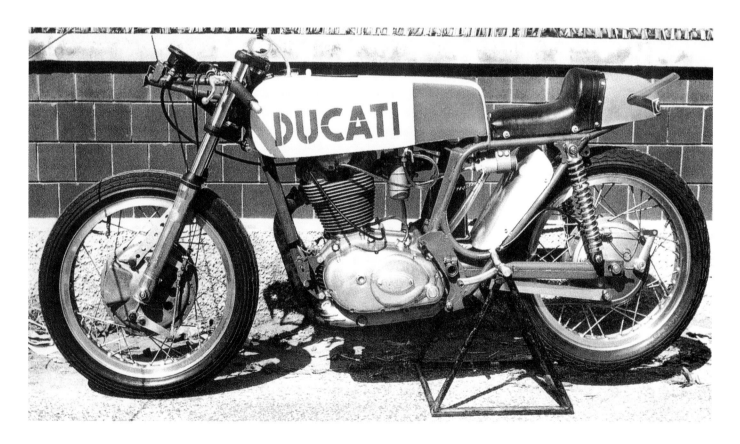

Spaggiari's 1970 450 racer was based on the production desmo and included a wet clutch.

PART 2

TWO HEADS ARE BETTER THAN ONE

CHAPTER 6

750 GT

1972 | 748cc air-cooled 90-degree twin | 80mm bore | 74.4mm stroke | 57hp at 7,700rpm | 408lb (185kg) | 118mph (190kmh)

After the difficult decade of the 1960s, Ducati approached the next decade under new management and with a much more positive outlook. The government controllers appointed Arnaldo Milvio and Fredmano Spairani to run the company, and the men were serious about entering the world of superbikes. In 1970 every rider dreamed of a superbike, and Milvio and Spairani wanted a large-displacement, high-performance bike for these enthusiasts. This was a big goal for a company that was a minor Italian manufacturer known primarily for producing smaller capacity singles and unremarkable two-strokes.

Ducati lacked the resources to create a three- or four-cylinder superbike such as those offered by Triumph and Honda, so chief engineer Fabio Taglioni was asked to design a 750 taking a pragmatic approach. Taglioni well remembered the racing success of the 120-degree 500cc Moto Guzzi twin of 1935 to 1953. This retained the horizontal front cylinder of a single, maintaining a lower center of gravity, with the rear cylinder angled slightly rearward. There were other advantages too, not the least being a good flow of air to cool the rear cylinder. These ideas influenced Taglioni when he took two existing 350cc singles and placed them on a common crankcase with the cylinders spaced 90 degrees apart.

Taglioni was an engineering purist and chose the 90-degree layout for several reasons. It offered the smoothness of perfect primary engine balance with only some high-frequency secondary imbalance. Also, the twin could be little wider than a single, keeping the engine low in the frame while maintaining good ground clearance. Taglioni called his layout an L-twin, and it established the engine layout that has been Ducati's trademark ever since.

The first production bike to carry Taglioni's new twin was the 750 GT. The bike's low-compression 8.5:1 pistons and Amal 30-millimeter carbs provided only moderate performance, but it was the manner in which the engine delivered that performance that was appealing. Power delivery was smooth and effortless, the engine relaxed and loping, even when running close to its 8,000-rpm redline. And there was a lot more to the 750 Ducati than just the engine. The handling was class leading. Taglioni eschewed the near universal double-cradle Norton Featherbed-style frame in favor of an open cradle design

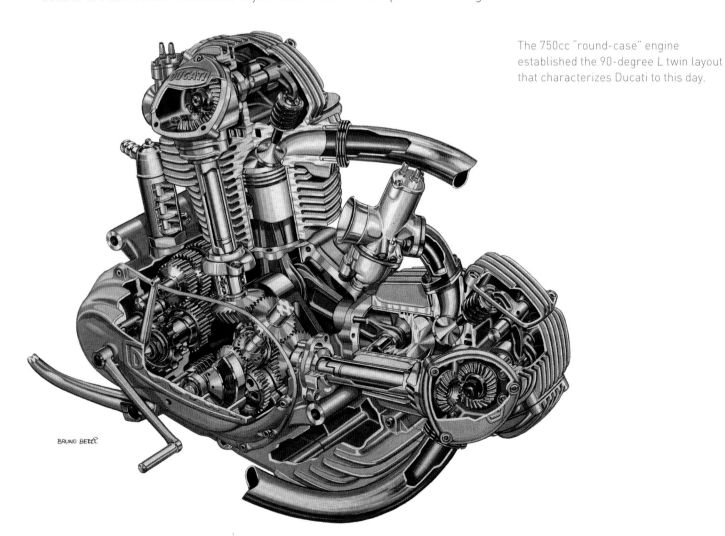

The 750cc "round-case" engine established the 90-degree L twin layout that characterizes Ducati to this day.

using the engine as a stressed member. While other superbikes had forks with skinny and flexible 35-millimeter tubes, the Ducati had a beefy 38-millimeter leading axle fork specially built by Marzocchi. The front brake included a cast-iron disc with a racing-style twin piston Lockheed caliper. Taglioni understood the benefit of minimizing unsprung weight, so the 750 GT ran on Borrani alloy rims, a 19-inch on the front and an 18-inch on the rear. At only 408 pounds (185 kilograms), the 750 GT was one of the lightest superbikes available.

The engine layout dictated a very long 1,530-millimeter wheelbase, and with an extreme steering rake of 29 degrees, the Ducati 750 provided unparalleled stability. It wasn't the most agile of superbikes, but when it came to high-speed handling the 750 Ducati was in a class of its own. This would pay dividends early in 1972 when Taglioni took a batch of GTs off the production line to prepare racing machines for the Imola 200.

The production 750 GT first appeared in July 1971, and many unique features characterized early examples. Their fiberglass gas tanks and side covers wore glittering '70s-style metalflake colors, stainless-steel Inox fenders covered the tires, some featured four-leading shoe rear brakes, and all had barking Conti exhaust systems. Ducati regarded the US market as particularly important for the 750, and the company built a specific US version with higher handlebars and a larger taillight. But the 750 GT was a slow seller until April 1972 when Paul Smart won the Imola 200 aboard a race-prepped version. As Ing. Fabio Taglioni observed in 1974, "When we won at Imola we won the market, too."

Over the next two years, the 750 GT gradually became more sanitized. Steel replaced fiberglass for the gas tank and side covers, painted steel mudguards took the place of the earlier stainless-steel units, and Italian Dell'Orto carburetors stood in for the original Amals. During 1973, Italian

Scarab brakes replaced the British Lockheed ones, and for 1974 the distinctive leading-axle fork made way for a Ceriani or Marzocchi center-axle type. Noise regulations saw ugly seamed Lafranconi silencers in place of the rowdy Contis, and eventually steel rims replaced the beautiful alloy Borranis. Considering production numbers were quite low, an astonishing number of 750 GT variants were made. A few even had an electric start.

The 750 GT concept may have been diluted by 1974, but the fabulous bevel-drive overhead camshaft "round-case" twin continued, at least for a short while. Characterized by distinctive polished aluminum outer engine covers, this wonderful engine ultimately met its demise due to its production costs. Its two overhead camshafts were driven by a set of bevel gears from the crankshaft and every shimmed gear was dependent on another, making this an extremely labor-intensive engine to manufacture. It was rumored that it took eight hours to assemble each production engine and two days for a racing variant. By 1974 the 750's proponents, Milvio and Spairani, had long departed, and the new bean counter, Cristiano de Eccher, saw no future for the expensive 750 in EFIM (Ente Finanzaria per gli Industrie Metalmeccaniche's) plans for Ducati. He hired car stylist Giorgetto Giugiaro of Italdesign to create the 750's replacement, the unloved 860 GT, at the same time abandoning the classic overhead camshaft singles for the disastrous parallel twins. The final nail in the coffin for the 750 round-case was US regulations from September 1974, which required all motorcycles to shift on the left side.

After a production life spanning only three years and a meager 5,284 units, the 750 GT and the distinctive round-case engine was finished. Today it is acknowledged as the father of the Ducati L-twin, and also the end of an era characterized by engineering purity and production without the interference of economic rationalization.

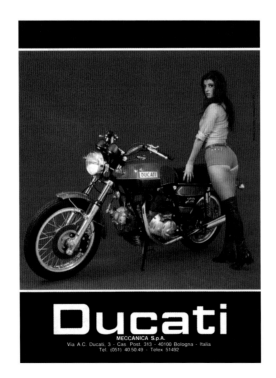

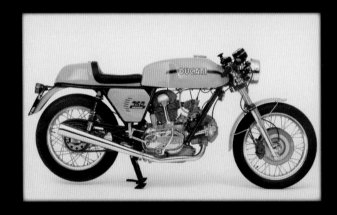

7 5 0   S P O R T

1973 | 748cc air-cooled 90-degree twin | 80mm bore | 74.4mm stroke | 62hp at 8,200rpm | 401lb (182kg) | 130mph (210kmh)

When Ing. Fabio Taglioni conceived the 750 Ducati in 1970 he always had it in his mind to develop the 750 into a sporting motorcycle. Ducatis were about sport and racing for Taglioni, and an early 750 prototype was fitted with 35-millimeter carburetors and spun to 9,500 rpm—a far cry from the eventual 750 GT. Other prototype 750 Sports had been displayed even before 1972's historic Imola victory. These were based on the GT but with clip-on handlebars, rear-set footpegs, and more highly tuned engines. After Imola, development began in earnest, and by mid-1972 the 750 Sport was in production.

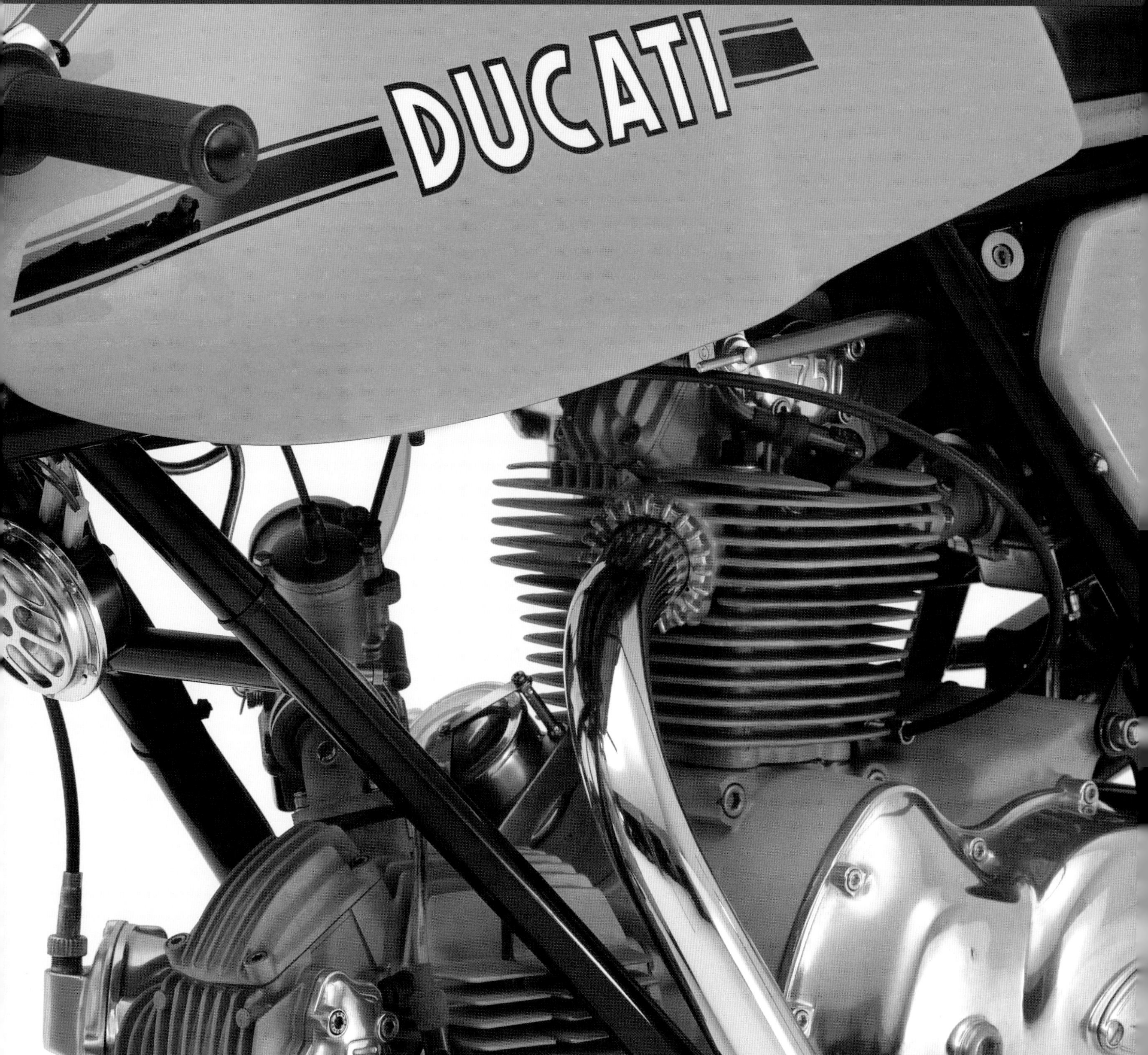
DUCATI
750
750

The 750 Sport epitomized the early 1970s factory café racer. If you wanted clip-on handlebars and rear-set footpegs, only Ducati and a couple of other Italian manufacturers offered that configuration. The solo seat made clear its purpose, and as a racer for the street, the 750 Sport was unchallenged. Ducati simply got it right with this motorcycle.

The first production 750 Sports of 1972 featured 750 GT-based frames with a wide rear subframe, minimalist Veglia instruments in separate pods, and a leading-axle Marzocchi fork with a single Lockheed front disc brake. The rear drum brake also carried over from the GT. The early 750 Sport had a distinctive "Z"-stripe color scheme, the striking yellow fiberglass bodywork accentuated by black engine covers. There was nothing subtle about the 750 Sport, and in the wake of the MV-beating performance of the 750 Desmos at Imola, customers expected improved performance. In this respect, the 750 Sport did not disappoint. With only minor engine modifications, the 750 Sport vied for best-performing 750 status—faster than most and probably the best handling.

Engine improvements over the 750 GT consisted purely of lighter, higher-compression (9.3:1) pistons matched to a correspondingly lighter crankshaft and larger carburetors fitted with velocity stacks. Although minor changes, the results were dramatic. The higher compression pistons better suited the radical GT camshaft profile, and new Dell'Orto PHF 32-millimeter "pumper"

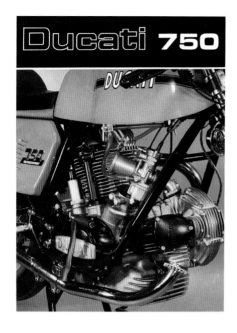

Although engine updates over the 750 GT were minimal, the 750 Sport offered much higher performance.

carburetors allowed the engine to breathe more freely. The difference in performance between a GT and Sport was considerable. The free-revving engine pulled smoothly and tractably from around 3,000 rpm all the way to its 8,000-rpm redline with virtually no vibration. The five-speed gearbox shifted accurately and smoothly despite the rear-set rods and linkages.

For 1973 the 750 Sport frame featured a narrower rear subframe and new bodywork. The styling and decals were similar to that of the yellow Desmo single. The long and narrow 1973 Sport looked stunning with its yellow fiberglass tank, seat, and matching fenders contrasting with the black-painted engine side covers. Most cycle parts were still identical to the GT, including Borrani aluminum wheel rims, single Scarab front disc brake, and Marzocchi suspension. The 1973 750 Sport was an uncompromised sporting motorcycle, still with no provision for a passenger or turn signals. The quality of the chrome and fiberglass may have been lacking, but the essentials were spot on.

In 1974, the 750 Super Sport entered production, displacing the 750 Sport as range leader. Changes in specification mirrored those of the GT. First were Ceriani center-axle forks with a single Brembo front disc, followed by a center-axle Marzocchi with Scarab brake. The gas tank was now steel in deference to the UK market, where the fiberglass tank was illegal. During 1974, polished aluminum engine cases replaced the black-painted cases. In an effort to improve the riding position, the widely splayed clip-on handlebars were now offset forward of the forks. This was a considerable improvement over the

The early 750 Sport was based on the 750 GT. The half fairing was an option.

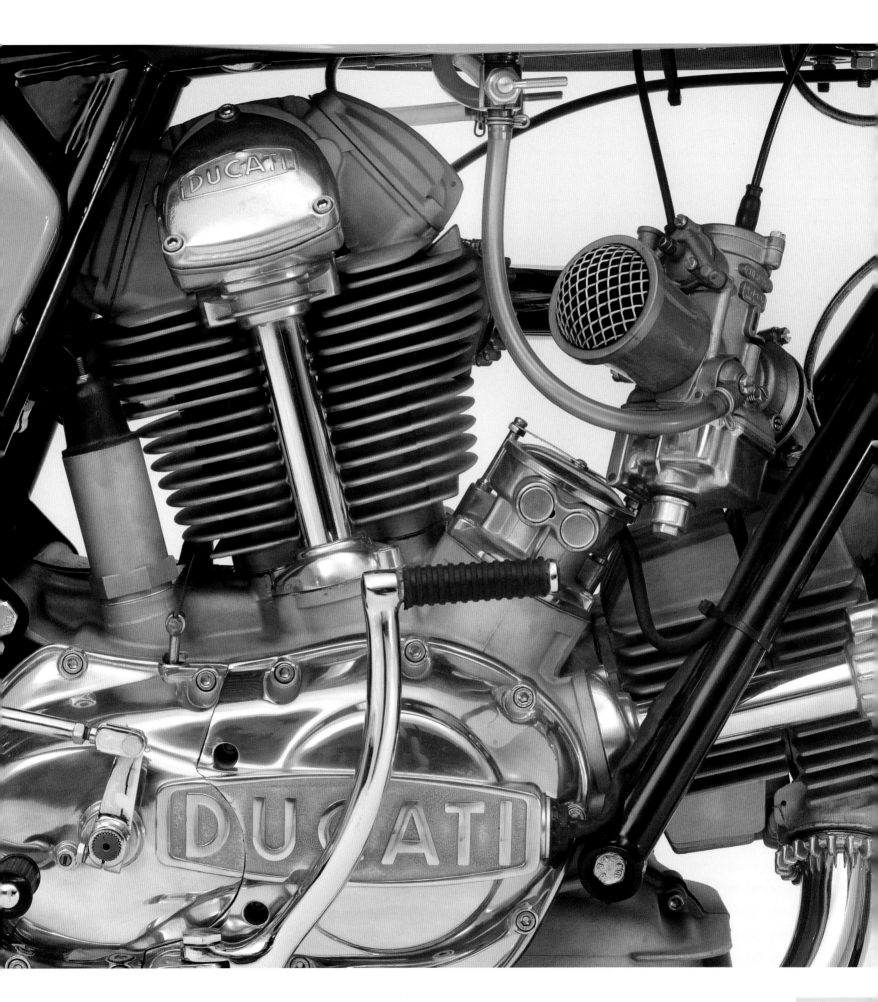

strange riding position of the earlier models, and it made the bike similar in feel to the 750 Super Sport. The switchgear and wiring mirrored the final 750 GTs and first 860s with boxy CEV items and a two-into-one throttle. The final 750 Sports also featured a dual seat as an option. US-bound models gained a larger taillight and turn signals. Compared to the final 750 Sports, the earlier versions were more minimalist and a purer display of the sporting concept.

Now matter which year produced, any 750 Sport was a superb sporting motorcycle. Its fiberglass bodywork made it lighter than the GT, and with more power it was a stronger performer. The brilliant handling mirrored that of the GT, but the 750 Sport's riding position lent itself to more spirited riding. In the real world, the 750 Sport was almost as fast as the revered 750 Super Sport, despite lacking the latter's desmodromic heads and 40-millimeter carburetors. To quote the June 1974 issue of *Cycle* magazine, "The 750 Sport has a great engine packaged with a brilliant chassis." *Cycle* went on to say, "The Ducati 750, in any of its three incarnations, is still the best handling street machine available." England's *Motorcyclist Illustrated* declared in July 1974, "The Ducati Sport stands level with the very best that history can offer to match it, and as a sporting machine probably better than almost any other big roadster in production."

Long, low, and narrow, the 750 Sport wasn't a motorcycle that you perched on top of, but one you molded into. It embodied the essence of mid-1970s sport motorcycling. The round-case 750 Sport epitomizes the very best of Ducati, providing uncompromised engine and chassis performance equal to the best in its day. And as with all 750 round-cases, 750 Sport production lasted only a few years and not many were made (1,625 total).

Ultimately the 750 Sport was overshadowed by the limited-production desmodromic 750 Super Sport. But as a pure sporting motorcycle, the 750 Sport deserves to stand alone as one of Ducati's greatest production machines.

CHAPTER 8

750 SUPER SPORT

1974 | 748cc air-cooled 90-degree twin | 80mm bore | 74.4mm stroke | 70hp at 9,000rpm | 397lb (180kg) | 143mph (230kmh)

On April 23, 1972, a brace of specially prepared desmodromic 750 racers took on the world's best and trounced them convincingly. The event was the inaugural Imola 200—the "Daytona of Europe" —for Formula 750 motorcycles, 750cc racing machines with production-based motors. The Imola win marked a transition for Ducati from relatively small, obscure Italian manufacturer of small-capacity singles to that of a marque equal to any other. Within Italy, and to certain cognoscenti in other countries, Fabio Taglioni and Ducati were known and respected for their technical excellence and innovation. But in production and sales terms, Ducati was a minor manufacturer. Imola forever changed that and signaled the beginning of a new era for Ducati.

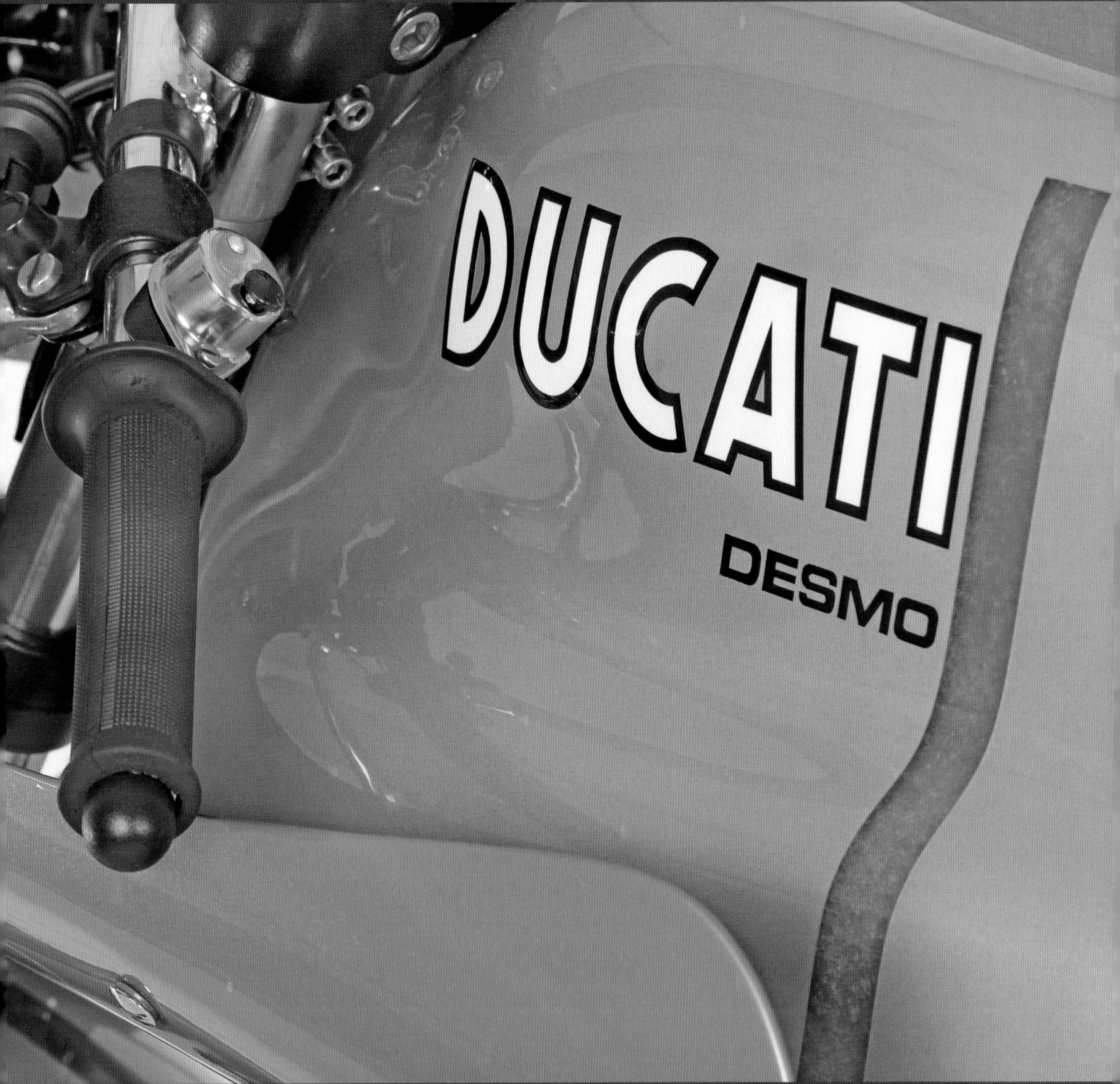
DUCATI
DESMO

Ducati transported the seven desmo racers in this distinctive glass-sided truck.

On race day, 70,000 spectators crammed into Autodromo Dino Ferrari at Imola. The field was filled with works machines from MV Agusta, Honda, Norton, Moto Guzzi, Triumph, and BSA, alongside factory-supported Kawasaki, Laverda, Suzuki, and BMW privateers. The Italian fans hoped to see the home factories beat the Japanese teams that had dominated Daytona. The best riders in the world were on hand to pilot these top-flight race bikes, including Giacomo Agostini, Phil Read, Roberto Gallina, Walter Villa, Ray Pickrell, Tony Jeffries, John Cooper, Percy Tait, Ron Grant, and Daytona winner Don Emde. Ducati arrived with seven desmodromic racers, its team lead by British rider Paul Smart and veteran Bruno Spaggiari.

The factory Ducatis had 750 GT-based frames (still with center stand mounts!), desmo cylinder heads, 40-millimeter Dell'Orto carburetors, dual-plug ignition, oil coolers, and triple Lockheed disc brakes. They reputedly produced 86 horsepower at 9,200 rpm. Imola's fast, sweeping curves—some smooth, others bumpy—and it's up-and-down topography seemed to suit the ultra-stable Ducatis.

Agostini on the MV Agusta led from the start, but after his retirement with 20 laps to go, Smart and Spaggiari had the race to themselves. Smart ultimately took the victory from Spaggiari, and the average race speed over 200 miles was an astonishing 97.76 miles per hour (157.35 km/h), with a fastest lap of 100.1 miles per hour (161.11 km/h) shared equally by Smart, Spaggiari, and Agostini.

After the race, Ducati promised Imola replicas, but these were slow to appear, and the 1973 Imola 200 came and went before any sign of a production 750 Desmo. For the 1973 Imola 200, Taglioni built three special short-stroke

Smart led Spaggiari to victory
on race day.

750cc racers, all with a shorter, lighter frame. On race day the Ducatis were
overshadowed by Jarno Saarinen on the Yamaha 351two-stroke, but Spaggiari
still managed a fine second place.

Preproduction 750 Super Sports began to trickle out of the factory late in
1973. One was shipped to *Cycle* magazine in California and became the basis
for Cook Neilson's famous California Hot Rod production racer. But it wasn't
until early 1974 that Ducati produced the one and only batch of round-case 750
Super Sports. Two hundred were built as homologation specials to satisfy FIM
regulations. Taglioni supervised production personally, seeing that 401 were
built so as to homologate the 750 SS for both 1974 and 1975.

The 750 Super Sport was the first factory replica of a race-winning
machine, and it was as close in specification to the Imola 200-winning racer
of 1972 as could be built and remain street legal. Only the barest concessions
were made for street use. The Conti mufflers provided minimal silencing,
and the 40-millimeter Dell'Ortos lacked air filters. There was no provision
for turn signals let alone an electric start. The quality of the fiberglass and
some of the ancillary components were of dubious quality, but the engine was

a masterpiece. A special computer-controlled Olivetti milling machine was installed at the factory to machine from billet each individual connecting rod, just as with the Imola racers, and all the rockers were highly polished. The 750 SS was the first Ducati twin with desmodromic valves and triple disc brakes, in this case Scarab on the front and Lockheed on the rear. Setting the 750 SS further apart was a 750 Sport-style "Azzurro"-painted frame and 18-inch Borrani alloy wheels in front and in rear. The frame color seemed to be chosen randomly from the range of outboard motors produced at Borgo Panigale at the time and has resulted in the nickname for the model as the "Green Frame."

No other contemporary machine offered comparable all-around performance. The power was modest, but so was the weight. As one of the first bikes to offer a factory fairing, its extremely narrow frontal area helped motivate the 750 SS to what was a very high top speed for the day. The combination of center-axle Marzocchi fork and 18-inch front wheel provided superior handling to the already excellent 750 GT and Sport.

For those who bought a 750 Super Sport, there was also the factory option

Taglioni and Smart after the
Imola victory.

of a racing kit. This comprehensive kit contained a full fairing and high-rise open megaphones, an oil cooler, higher lift "Imola" desmodromic camshafts, a selection of rear sprockets, and a range of main jets. For engines fitted with the Imola camshafts but still with Conti silencers, the maximum revs increased from 8,800 rpm to 9,000 rpm. With the megaphones, revs increased to 9,200 rpm.

However, even as the 750 SS was being produced, the round-case engine series was being phased out in favor of the Giugiaro-inspired square-case 860. Economics and forthcoming legislation regarding noise and left side gear shifting would leave the 750 SS of 1974 as the only desmodromic version of the round-case engine, and one of the rarest and most special of all production street Ducatis. It also represented the end of an era for a certain type of production engine, an era where cost and government legislation had minimal influence on design and execution. As a racing bike with lights and a horn, the 750 SS was a perfect example of form following function, the successful aesthetics not the result of stylists, but of subconscious evolution.

9 0 0 N C R

1978 | 864cc air-cooled 90-degree twin | 86mm bore | 74.4mm stroke | 92hp at 8,500rpm | 353lb (160kg) | 155mph (250kmh)+

For Ducati's great engineer Fabio Taglioni, racing was pivotal to success. He grew up in a world where Italian manufacturers dominated on the track, and he believed Ducati should emulate the success of Moto Guzzi, Gilera, and MV Agusta. Unfortunately, Ducati's status as a government-owned company meant its management was fluid and often unsupportive. There was no guarantee management was even interested in motorcycles, let alone racing. After 1973, new general manager Cristiano de Eccher actively discouraged racing, so Taglioni and his department decided to develop racing machines unofficially through a subsidiary, NCR.

NCR was established as a specialist race shop back in 1967 by three factory mechanics: Giorgio Nepoti, Rino Caracchi, and Rinaldo Rizzi. They set up in via Signorini 16, close to the factory at Borgo Panigale, but soon Rizzi left and the operation became Nepoti Caracchi Racing (NCR). After Ducati's success at Montjuich in 1973, Fabio Taglioni was determined to persevere with a racing program. Without managerial support, teaming up with old friends seemed the obvious solution. Taglioni wanted to win the 1975 FIM Coupe d'Endurance, and running on a shoestring budget, with machines entered through the NCR banner, he very nearly succeeded.

The 1976 NCR endurance racers were the first to feature the distinctive one-piece tank and seat.

NCR endurance racers surprised many pundits by winning the first two events in 1975: Montjuich and Mugello. Without full factory backing, the Ducatis struggled throughout the season, but Benjamin Grau eventually finished third in the championship. This promising result inspired an increased endurance effort for 1976, and the NCR machines became even more specialized. In their details, they were pure works of art. Caracchi was a master machinist and created beautiful components for even such simple devices as the rear brake caliper support. Nepoti was responsible for the NCR's bulletproof crankshaft. Now with factory support, they created spectacular endurance racing machines, these sharing virtually nothing with any production Ducati.

By 1976 Franco Zauibouri had replaced de Eccher as general manager, and with him came a more positive attitude towards racing. In a bid to win the Coupe d'Endurance, Zauibouri sanctioned the unofficial development of endurance racers. Though these machines were entered by NCR, they were factory racers. The increased budget was immediately apparent in the improved presentation of the machines. Sadly the bikes proved too fragile to win the Coupe d'Endurance, falling to Honda's onslaught. The same fate befell the NCR racers for 1977. The lineup of five NCR machines was impressive, but the bikes proved no match for Honda's RCB.

Taglioni still wanted to compete in the Coupe d'Endurance, but he knew that in this highly competitive series the Ducatis would never best the might of Honda. The introduction of the Tourist Trophy Formula 1 race for production-based machinery at the Isle of Man would provide the venue he needed. Formula 1 required that the engine stroke be retained, but there were few restrictions regarding engine and chassis modifications. Taglioni reasoned that he could run nearly endurance-specification machines in TT F1 and that the 900 NCR would surely prove competitive. Ducati signed Mike Hailwood for the 1978 TT F1, providing the impetus to produce a small number of 900 NCR Formula One machines.

Unlike the endurance racers, the Formula 1 900 NCRs were catalogued models. They carried 900 SS engine numbers but featured specially cast crankcases incorporating a spin-on oil filter, and they retained the earlier 750 bevel-drive layout with battery, coil, and points ignition. The engine displacement was the same as the production 900 SS (864cc), also with an 80-degree included valve angle. Engine updates included larger valves (44-millimeter intake and 38-millimeter exhaust), lighter 10:1 Borgo pistons, 12-millimeter lift desmodromic camshafts, and a lightened crankshaft. The F1 900 NCR also featured a close ratio gearbox, straight-cut primary gears, a dry clutch, and Dell'Orto 40-millimeter carburetors.

The Daspa frame weighed a scant 26.5 pounds (12 kilograms), but the suspension, wheels, and brakes were less exotic than on the endurance machines. Cavazzi's quick-release wheel system and milled brake caliper mount were absent, as were the magnesium forks and shock absorbers. The wheels were magnesium Campagnolo, and nice touches included vernier adjustment for the milled foot levers and a one-piece fiberglass tank and seat in the traditional NCR colors of red and silver.

Steve Wynne of Sports Motorcycles in Manchester, England, signed Mike Hailwood for the 1978 TT Formula 1, and he received two NCR 900s, one for Hailwood and one for Roger Nicholls. Wynne had the bikes painted in Castrol's colors of red, white, and green. Hailwood won the race in a fairytale comeback, cruising to the finish at an average speed of 108.51 miles per hour. His fastest lap was a blistering 110.62 miles per hour. It was an astounding victory and vindication of the 900 NCR's brilliant balance of power and handling. The Isle of Man success would be pivotal in the racing history of Ducati, just as the Imola win had been in 1972. It was Ducati's first World Championship, and the legendary Mike Hailwood was its first World Champion.

Ducati was so pleased with the 1978 result that it decided to support an official team for the 1979 Formula 1 and Classic TT. TT F1 regulations now required the engine to be based on the standard square-case 900 SS, while the

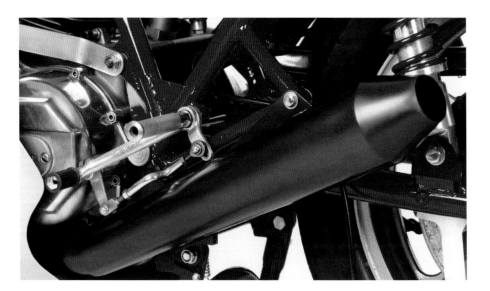

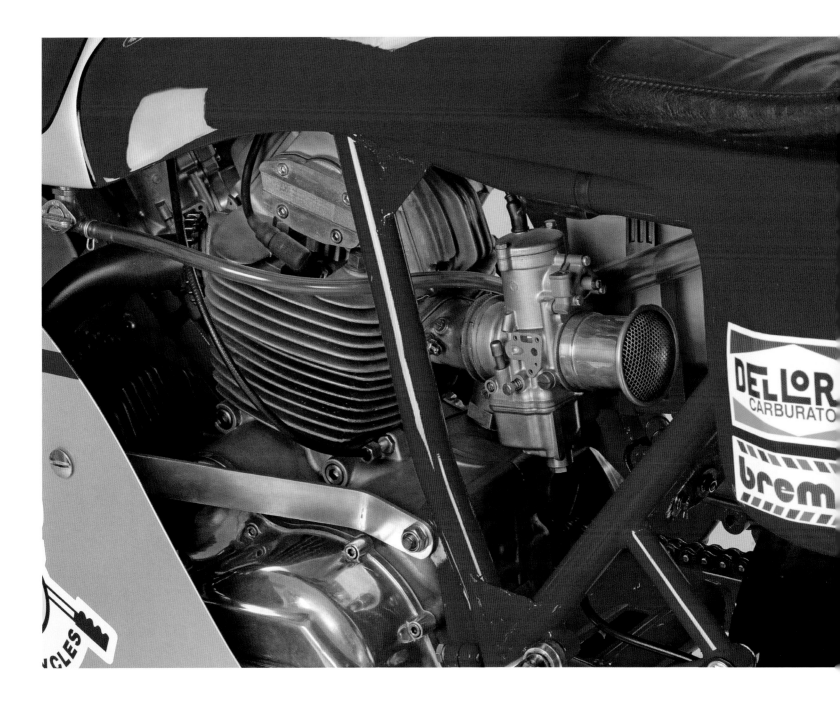

Classic TT racer featured an endurance-type engine with special crankcases and dry clutch. The bikes were disappointing however, and Hailwood could only manage fifth in the TT F1 race. George Fogarty (Carl's father) rode the Classic machine, as Hailwood refused to race it.

Although the new 900 NCR Formula 1 machines were the most successful NCR racers, NCR continued to develop endurance machines. While these were spectacularly beautiful, they were unreliable. The final victory for the NCR 900 was in 1980 when Jose Mallol and Alejandro Tejedo won the Barcelona 24-hour race at Montjuich. By 1981 the emerging Superbike class had overtaken Formula 1, and the bevel-drive twin was simply uncompetitive. The 900 NCR is one of the most beautiful Ducatis ever and remains a testament to the creativity and artistry of the engineers who designed and built it.

CHAPTER 10

9 0 0   S U P E R   S P O R T

1980 | 864cc air-cooled 90-degree twin | 86mm bore | 74.4mm stroke | 57hp at 7,400rpm | 452lb (205kg) | 124mph (200kmh)

The seeds for the creation of the 900 Super Sport were sown as early as June 1973, when Fabio Taglioni prepared an 860 version of the 750 Super Sport for the Barcelona 24-hour race at Montjuic Park. While not as high-profile an event as the Imola 200, this was still a very significant victory for Ducati. Salvador Canellas and Benjamin Grau won at a record average speed of 71 miles per hour (114.3 km/h).

The first 900 Super Sport appeared in 1975.

Early 1974 saw the production of the one series of 750 Super Sports, and by the end of the year the new angular Giugiaro-designed 860 GT had superseded the 750 GT. With the passing of the 750 SS, Ducati needed a sport bike in the lineup, a role fulfilled by the 900 Super Sport of 1975. This bike would go on to become one of the greatest of all Ducati production models.

Because production of the 750cc round-case engine had ceased, the basis of the 900 SS engine was the new 860cc square-case. Inside the bevel-drive engine were dual-ribbed forged connecting rods and higher compression 86-millimeter pistons. Desmodromic heads topped the cylinders, and the engine breathed through a pair of unfiltered 40-millimeter Dell'Orto carburetors. Like the 860, spark was provided by the problematic Ducati Elettrotecnica electronic ignition system.

Apart from the engine, the 900 Super Sport owed more to the 1974 750 Super Sport than the 860 GT. The frame was nearly identical, as were the 18-inch Borrani wheels and Marzocchi suspension. Updates over the previous 750 Super Sport included Brembo brakes with drilled discs. The early 900 Super Sports remained true to the purist bloodline, with a fiberglass gas tank, solo seat, no turn signals, right side gearshift, and the traditional Conti silencers. Only 246 1975 900 Super Sports were built, and they expanded the performance parameters established by the round-case 750 SS, providing similar handling but with more power.

The first 900 Super Sport was immediately successful on the road and track, but the specification (fiberglass tank, right-side shift, open carbs, etc.) didn't allow it to be sold in many countries, including the United States. While the ugly 860 GT sat unsold in showrooms and warehouses, dealers were crying out for 900 Super Sports. In response to demand, the 900 Super Sport was modified for 1976 so that it could meet noise and emission requirements worldwide, and in so doing it became Ducati's savior.

The 900 Super Sport internal engine specifications remained largely unchanged for 1976 and 1977. Updates to the rest of the bike included a left-side gearshift, right-side rear brake, and a quieter intake and exhaust system. Dell'Orto PHF 32A carburetors with air cleaners replaced the 40-millimeter carbs, but the larger carbs remained as an option. Stricter noise regulations meant the 860 GT's Lafranconis replaced the Contis, but the earlier mufflers were available as an option.

While the silver frame, Borrani wheels, and Brembo brakes were much as before, a steel gas tank replaced the fiberglass version. A dual seat was also an option. Completing the new specification were an updated instrument panel, switches, and turn signals. Unfortunately, the quest to produce a universal Super Sport resulted in a flawed creation. The essence was there, but some of the details were ill conceived. One thing was certain, though: the 900 Super Sport still provided class-leading performance and handling.

By 1978 the 900 square-case engine had evolved into the updated version powering the new Darmah and featuring an improved crankshaft (with 38-millimeter crankpin and needle rollers), Bosch ignition (with stepped advance), and the left-side gearshift incorporated behind the clutch. These improvements soon appeared on the 900 Super Sport, initially in the traditional blue and silver with Borrani wheels.

Shortly before Mike Hailwood's 1978 TT F1 victory at the Isle of Man, Ducati built a limited-edition black and gold 900 Super Sport with Speedline magnesium wheels specifically for the British market. Following the success of the UK limited edition, the black and gold color scheme with gold alloy wheels replaced the traditional silver and blue, with wire-spoked wheels for 1979. Unlike the UK edition that had unique hand-painted gold stripes, the stripes on the 1979 and 1980 900 SS mirrored those of the earlier blue and silver

bikes. Six-spoke aluminum FPS wheels replaced the magnesium five-spoke Speedline wheels following problems with cracks and corrosion. Some 1980 900 Super Sports had 280-millimeter drilled brake discs with alloy carriers and were clamped by Brembo Gold Series brake calipers. Most had a dual seat and were specified with 32-millimeter carbs and the quieter Lafranconi or Silentium silencers. Contis and 40-millimeter Dell'Ortos remained an option as in past practice. For many, the 1979–1980 black and gold 900 Super Sport embodies the finest attributes of the line. The engine, with the Bosch ignition and improved gearshift, was the smoothest and most reliable, while the black bodywork contrasting with gold-painted wheels was an aesthetic triumph. After two years, Ducati decided it was time to update the 900 Super Sport, and a new model appeared for 1981. Most of the changes were cosmetic, but there was also a decline in quality as the VM Group management strove to increase production. At the time, much of the Borgo Panigale plant was used to build diesel engines for the current owners, and the motorcycle division was under increasing pressure to improve profitability.

The silver paint of the 1981 model was designed to replicate the earlier 900 Super Sport, but the dual seat was a new design. The black frame and gold FPS wheels carried over from the black and gold SS, but somehow the styling didn't gel as it had with earlier versions. Production ended during 1982. By now the kick-start-only Super Sport was an anachronism.

Production totaled 6,103 bikes over eight years, and the 900 Super Sport now has earned the status as the classic bevel-drive twin-cylinder Ducati. It may not be particularly rare, and the 900 Super Sport may have had its share of reliability problems, but no other serial-production Ducati sums up the sporting essence of the marque better than this motorcycle.

Ducati's success at Barcelona was repeated in 1975.

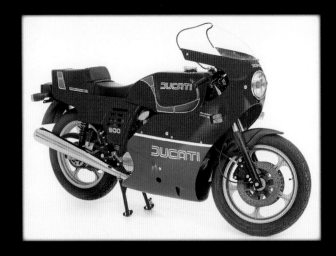

CHAPTER 11

MIKE HAILWOOD REPLICA

1984 | 864cc air-cooled 90-degree twin | 86mm bore | 74.4mm stroke | 72hp at 7,000rpm | 468.5lb (212.5kg) | 138mph (222kmh)

The success of the "Imola" replica 750 Super Sport of 1974 had shown Ducati the marketing benefits of race replicas to the sales of an entire range of motorcycles. Though the 750 SS was reasonably successful in production racing—culminating in Cook Neilson's stunning victory in the 1977 Daytona Superbike landmark race— victories were rare for Ducati in the 1970s. That all changed in 1978 when legendary racer Mike Hailwood came out of retirement at age 38 to race an NCR Ducati and win the Formula 1 race at the Isle of Man.

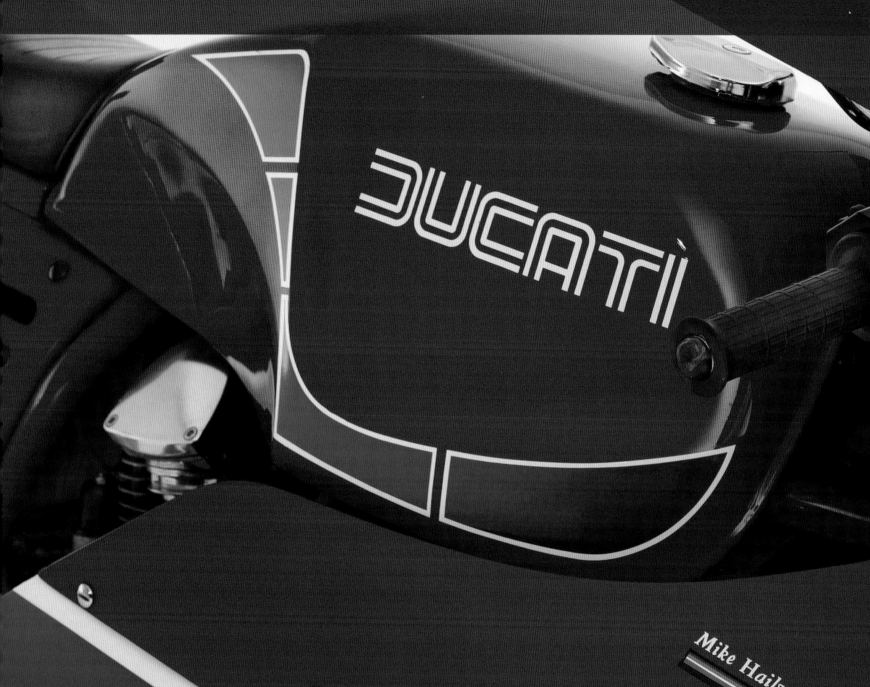

Mike Hailwood replica

Within a year of Hailwood's triumph, a production Mike Hailwood Replica (MHR) appeared at the London Motorcycle Show. By this point, some of the momentum of Hailwood's 1978 win had been lost, as he had had a miserable race in the 1979 Formula One TT. Still, Ducati moved forward with its replica. Ultimately its decision proved correct, as the MHR would become Ducati's most successful model over the next few years.

Ducati took many more liberties with the term "replica" than it had with the 1974 Super Sport. This was reflected in the first documentation related to the Mike Hailwood Replica, as the factory statement was almost apologetic for the bike's rather unremarkable specification. "It does not represent a new design," began Ducati's press release, "since even if the factory made a true reproduction of the T.T. machine, the strict and rigorous race regulations imposed by the English authorities for this class must be followed." Due to these regulations, the cycle parts and engine were identical to the 900 Super Sport, and the Mike Hailwood Replica was initially a cosmetic variation of that machine. The first series was produced primarily for the UK market, each coming with a certificate of authenticity.

The MHR's bodywork is what really set the replica apart from its 900 Super Sport stablemate. This was the first production Ducati factory-fitted with a full fairing. Patterned on Hailwood's 1979 NCR Formula One Ducati rather than the more successful 1978 bike, the fiberglass, full racing-style fairing was red, white, and green, the same Castrol colors as Hailwood's TT-winning Sports Motorcycles 900 NCR. Evidence that the Hailwood Replica was hastily conceived was indicated by the 18-liter 900 Super Sport fuel tank hiding beneath a fiberglass cover. Initially Ducati planned to include a fiberglass fuel

Mike Hailwood came out of retirement in 1978 to ride an NCR 900 in the TT Formula 1 at the Isle of Man. He won the race at record speed.

tank with an Imola-style clear strip, but with fiberglass fuel tanks banned in the United Kingdom, this makeshift solution was adopted.

The first 200 Hailwood Replicas were constructed in September 1979, and the next series was essentially the same but for a few bodywork updates, notably a properly constructed steel gas tank. Production of the second series of 900 Replicas commenced in the latter part of 1979 and continued into 1980. By the end of 1980, only around 550 Replicas had been built, so Ducati decided it was time to up the ante. Ducati sales were flat in 1980 despite the introduction of the all-new Pantah, but Hailwood's TT win remained fresh in the minds of many enthusiasts. So for 1981 Ducati focused on increasing production and improving practicality mostly through cosmetic updates.

Tragically, Mike Hailwood died in an automobile accident in March of that year. Despite this, the factory decided to continue with the production of the Mike Hailwood Replica. It would remain the flagship of Ducati's range until 1985.

For 1981 and 1982, the 900 MHR featured a two-piece fairing and side covers to hide the battery and rear carburetor. Although the new fairing was a boon for maintenance (the oil could now be changed without removing the entire fairing), all MHRs remained 900 SS-based and kick-start only. The performance was dulled slightly by quieter Silentium mufflers, though most owners retro-fitted a set of barking Contis as soon as they took delivery. Throughout 1981 and 1982, most bevel twins built by Ducati were 900 MHRs.

The unremarkable 900 S2 replaced the 900 Super Sport during 1982, but the 900 Hailwood Replica continued essentially unchanged for 1983. These remained kick-start only, and they were the final series of bikes based on the 900 Super Sport.

Early in 1983, the factory began work to update the MHR. Though the kick-start Hailwood had been the mainstay of Ducati's bevel-drive lineup, the days of kick-start only motorcycles were numbered. Because the electric starter

Ducati continued trading on Hailwood's victory even as late as 1982.

required a larger battery, the new MHR was based on the 900 S2 rather than the earlier Super Sport. These final 900s were the smoothest and best developed of all the 864cc engines—their smoothness rivaling that of the earlier 750cc engine, and the production and quality at the factory was much more consistent than it had been even a year earlier.

The engine update was the most comprehensive since the square-case redesign of 1974. New crankcases included an oil-level sight glass and a spin-on oil filter, and the shape of both engine side covers was restyled away from the angular Giugiaro square-case type. The cylinders and liners were now in one piece and were coated with Gilnisil to reduce wear. Further updates included a hydraulically actuated dry clutch and a small Nippon Denso electric starter motor.

The new 900 MHR was heavier, longer, and taller than its predecessor and shared few cycle parts despite the factory claiming otherwise. The fairing was narrower and taller, and the dash lights and controls updated. The Oscam wheels now accepted tubeless tires. The S2-derived frame was something of a step backwards, however, and inferior to the SS type.

The 1984 900 Mike Hailwood Replica was a stopgap model while Fabio Taglioni and his new assistant, Massimo Bordi, developed a new engine. Well before the 1983 agreement that led to Ducati's acquisition by Cagiva, then-current ownership (the VM Group) had given Taglioni the go-ahead to revamp the bevel-gear engine. The updated engine finally materialized in mid-1984, and was visually identical to the revised 900. When placed in the chassis of the 1984 900 MHR, it was difficult to distinguish between the two. However, inside the Mille engine there were numerous important changes, which contributed to the engine's markedly different personality. Without question, the Mille engine was the most developed of all the bevel-drive twins and arguably the finest. It was certainly the strongest.

Increased bore and stroke saw engine capacity grow to 973cc. The bore was only increased 2 millimeters to 88 millimeters, but the stroke increased to 80 millimeters. The crankshaft followed Pantah practice and was forged in one piece with two-piece plain big-end bearings and bolted up connecting rods. Other updates extended to a revised primary drive and an all-new gearbox. Inside the cylinder head were larger valves, but the traditional 80-degree valve angle remained.

Production of the Mille Mike Hailwood Replica ended in early 1986 soon after Cagiva took over Ducati. Ultimately the MHR was seen as a dinosaur, its twin-shock chassis rooted in the 1970s and its expensive engine uneconomic to produce in large numbers. Mike Hailwood's spectacular Isle of Man victory had lived on for eight years, but Ducati was about to embark on a new, and even more successful, era.

CHAPTER 12

500 SL PANTAH

1980 | 498cc air-cooled 90-degree twin | 74mm bore | 58mm stroke | 50hp at 9,050rpm | 403lb (183kg) | 124mph (200kmh)

The 1970s was another decade distinguished by poor management and dubious marketing moves. The year 1974 saw the end of the singles and round-case 750s, replaced by the ungainly 860 and an unremarkable parallel twin. In 1976, when Ducati's management finally realized that the parallel twins were a commercial disaster, legend has it that Ing. Fabio Taglioni smiled, reached into his bottom drawer, and presented full technical drawings for a 500cc V-twin engine.

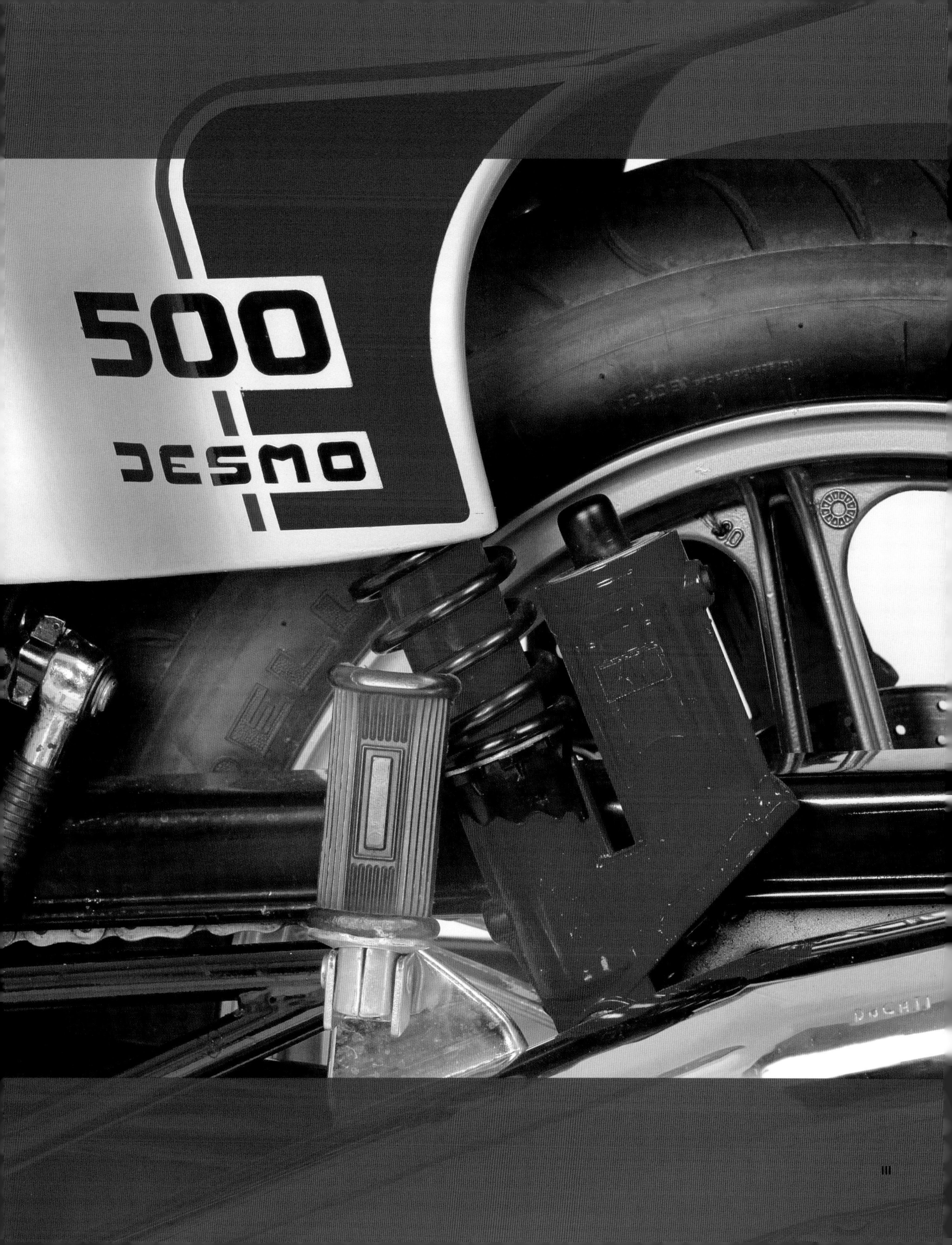
500
DESMO

Camshaft drive by toothed rubber belts rather than the traditional bevel gears ensured this new engine would be both cheaper to manufacture than the bevel-drive engines and quieter running as well. This design—the Pantah—is also Taglioni's most enduring, having begun its production life in 1979. Over that time it has grown from 498cc to 1,078cc and spawned an entire range of sophisticated four-valve Ducatis. No other Ducati engine has had so much influence on the direction of the company. So superior was the Pantah engine in terms of reliability and cost effectiveness that within six years it was the only engine produced by the company. The Pantah engine single-handedly changed the perception of Ducatis and their reliability. With Ducatis once considered idiosyncratic and only for enthusiasts prepared to spend time maintaining their machinery, the Pantah brought the Ducati legend to a far wider audience. Taglioni saved the day yet again.

The Pantah could have gone into production almost immediately, but at the time Taglioni first showed it, the EFIM management was in turmoil. Between 1977 and 1978, motorcycle production at Borgo Panigale nearly halved, dropping from 7,167 to 4,436—partly due to a decline in the US market, but also because of Ducati's unsatisfactory model range. In July 1978, control of Ducati passed to another group, Finmeccanica, within the VM Group. This proved a dubious move for Ducati as Finmeccanica was heavily involved in the production of diesel engines and it was reluctant to increase motorcycle production. By 1979 however, Fabio Taglioni was finally allowed to put his new engine and motorcycle into production.

While the range of bevel-gear twins remained strongly influenced by the singles throughout their lifespan, the Pantah combined the past with the

During 1980, the factory prepared a few racing Pantahs. These 70-horsepower machines had NCR-replica bodywork.

present. Its roots were in the 1971–1973 500cc Grand Prix V-twin racers, the 90-degree twin cylinder layout retaining the racer's vertically split crankcases, but with the Pantah's swingarm now pivoting on bearings within the gearbox casing. The idea was to bring the swingarm pivot as close as possible to the countershaft sprocket, thus reducing chain snatch. In many ways, the Pantah was a mirror image of the larger twins with the helical primary drive gears on the right side and the alternator on the left. In the interests of improving reliability, a forged one-piece crankshaft with two-piece connecting rods and plain-bearing big ends replaced the problematic pressed-together roller bearing crank of the bevel-drive engines. This was a significant update, and big-end problems became a thing of the past. The two-valve cylinder heads featured a more up-to-date 60-degree included valve angle, and all versions had desmodromic valve actuation. Feeding these cylinder heads was a pair of large (for a 500) 36-millimeter Dell'Orto PHF carburetors. A huge air cleaner and restrictive mufflers strangled the engine, so early 500s had to be revved hard to unleash the available performance. But unlike the bevel-drive engines, Pantahs didn't self-destruct if over-revved.

A trellis-type frame consisted of two pairs of parallel tubes running from the rear cylinder to the steering head, meeting another pair of tubes running up from the rear of the crankcases. The engine hung below the trellis and was bolted at six points. While the frame wasn't exceptionally rigid, it still provided the Pantah with sure-footed handling. It wasn't the most compact frame however, as the wheelbase was still a rangy 1,450 millimeters, but this was considerably shorter than the larger displacement twins. Suspension was by Marzocchi in front and rear, with a skinny 35-millimeter diameter fork and the usual limp shocks. The triple-disc brakes were also smaller than those fitted to the larger twins, with 260-millimeter discs and small 05 series Brembo brake calipers at both ends.

When the first production Pantah appeared in 1980, the styling didn't meet with universal acclaim. Those first 500 SL bikes were unlike other V-twin Ducatis in that they had very little bottom end and midrange power. They also lacked the rowdy mechanical note of the bevel twins—their toothed-belt camshaft drive, rubber plugs between the cylinder fins, and restrictive Conti silencers all conspiring to make the Pantah uncharacteristically quiet for a Ducati.

Racers Vanes Francini, Paolo Menchini, and Guido Del Piano successfully campaigned 600cc race-kitted Pantahs in the Italian National Junior Championship, ensuring that the 500 SL would grow into a 600. This happened in 1981, a simple 80-millimeter overbore creating the 600 SL. Power increased to 61 horsepower at 9,100 rpm. While the chassis remained much as before, a silver and red color scheme set it apart from the pale blue 500. Beginning in 1982, the 600 SL was also available in the red/white/green Mike Hailwood Replica colors.

During this period, Tony Rutter was virtually invincible on the factory TT2, winning four consecutive World Championships between 1981 and 1984. When the FIM Endurance World Championship rules increased displacement to 750cc for 1984, Ducati felt it could be competitive with a Pantah-based 750 racer. Thus the 650 SL was born, purely to homologate the 61.5-millimeter stroke for the 750 TT1. The 650 finally grew to 750 with the 1985 750 F1. In the meantime, a range of dubious offspring grew out of the Pantah: the 350 XL, the 350 SL, and the particularly ugly 350 and 600 TL. The SL Pantah may not have been the world's most beautiful design, but the TL's designers obviously penned it after a Friday lunch break.

The Pantah lived on as the 350 and 650 Cagiva Alazzurra through 1987, and even today all the small-capacity two-valve Ducati engines are based strongly on that first 500. Its central design features influence the entire current engine lineup, except the Superquadro. Taglioni may be no longer be with us, but his legacy continues.

CHAPTER 13

750 F1 MONTJUICH

1986 | 748cc air-cooled 90-degree twin | 88mm bore | 61.5mm stroke | 95hp at 10,000rpm | 342lb (155kg) | 143mph (230kmh)

The new SL Pantah was a commendable design, but as a racing machine, it had its limitations. Fabio Taglioni addressed this issue for the 1981 racing season, releasing his tour de force, the TT2. This brilliant design was successful from the outset, and Sauro Pazzaglia proved the point by winning its race debut at Misano in March. The factory provided Tony Rutter a similar machine later in the year for the Ulster race, and with it he sealed the first of his four TT2 World Championships.

Two factory TT2s at the start of an Italian Formula 2 Championship race in 1981. Massimo Broccoli (#2) won the series that year.

The TT2 marked the first official factory return to competition since 1975. Except for the basic engine architecture, the race bike shared little with any production model. Taglioni designed a completely new frame, weighing a mere 15.4 pounds (7 kilograms), and a single-cantilever Paioli shock absorber provided the rear suspension. The compact and heavily triangulated frame was made of essentially straight tubes. The engine served as a stressed member, helping to keep the weight down to a feathery 269 pounds (122 kilograms). The bike was also extremely compact with only a 55-inch (1,395-millimeter) wheelbase. With claimed power of 76 horsepower at 10,750 rpm, this effective racer expressed the Taglioni tradition of achieving maximum results through a balance of power and weight. It was light, athletic, slim, and had a wide powerband.

In 1984 both the TT1 and the World Endurance Championship were restricted to 750cc, thus providing impetus for the creation of the 750cc TT1. Ducati ran a factory-prepared prototype TT1 in July 1983 at Barcelona's Montjuich Park, where in the hands of Benjamin Grau, Enrique de Juan, and Luis Reyes it won the annual 24-hour race by completing 708 laps to the second-place Kawasaki's 690. This success led to factory entries in several 1984 endurance events, but good results were difficult to come by. Ducati persevered for 1985, modifying the TT1 with 16-inch wheels, a 42-millimeter Marzocchi fork, and linkage rising-rate rear suspension, and output of more than 90 horsepower. Unfortunately, limited resources meant good results remained elusive.

Cagiva acquired Ducati in 1985, immediately resulting in a more serious racing program. The 1986 season started well with Marco Lucchinelli winning the Battle of the Twins race at Daytona in March on an experimental 851cc 750 F1-based racer. Lucchinelli also won the Battle of the Twins race at Laguna

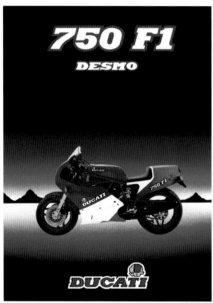

Seca and won the opening round of the World TT Formula 1 Championship at Santamonica, Misano. At the Barcelona 24-hour race in October, Juan Garriga, Carlos Cardus, and the steadfast Benjamin Grau won with the 851cc TT1.

Though the TT2 and TT1 were achieving considerable racing success, it wasn't until 1985 that a production version, the 750 F1, appeared. While reasonably faithful to the factory racer, it was compromised in its details, as was often the case with production Ducatis at this time. Small 500cc Pantah valves restricted the 750cc engine's breathing, and some of the styling was awkward. Basic Marzocchi suspension and the combination of 16-inch front and 18-inch rear wheels compromised the 750 F1's handling. Still, compared to the final bevel-drive Milles and the SL Pantah, the F1 was a generation ahead when it came to steering and handling. The F1's low weight and short wheelbase made it a surprisingly quick road bike, considering its lowish power output. Just like the magnificent TT1 and TT2 racers, it managed to match much more powerful bikes with its better balance and wider powerband.

A significantly improved 750 F1 appeared for 1986. Engine updates included stronger crankcases, crankshaft, and gearbox; larger valves; and a hydraulically operated dry clutch. Suspension was improved with an adjustable 40-millimeter Forcella Italia fork. To commemorate the 1983 24-hour race victory at Barcelona, a higher specification, limited-edition race replica was created based on the 750 F1. The 750 F1 Montjuich was a race replica that reflected the finest tradition of Ducati's limited-edition models. The Montjuich was much more highly tuned than the F1, with hotter camshafts, Dell'Orto PHM40ND carburetors, and a less-restrictive Verlicchi two-into-one "Riservato Competizione" exhaust system. Rear suspension was still via

a simple cantilever, but the swingarm was an aluminum Verlicchi item, and both front and rear wheels were 16-inch, much like the factory TT1 racers. The wheels were special lightweight composite Marvics with magnesium hubs and spokes bolted to Akront aluminum rims. Rim sizes were much wider than the standard F1 at 3.50x16 and 4.25x16, and they were shod with Michelin racing tires. Other detail differences included an aluminum fuel tank, four-piston Brembo "Gold Line" racing calipers with fully floating discs all round (280 millimeters at the front and 260 millimeters in rear), a vented dry clutch, and a racing-style front fender. The relationship between the Montjuich and F1 was similar to that which existed between the original 1974 750 Super Sport and 750 Sport: a limited production bike that offered higher performance through engine modifications, better brakes, and less weight. Unlike the original 750 SS, the Montjuich was created and sold as a limited-edition item, each of the 200 bikes having a numbered plaque on the gas tank.

By 1986 the Cagiva takeover was well in effect, and the new management was anxious to promote both Cagiva and Ducati in the United States. The 1987 F1 race replica was named the Laguna Seca in honor of Marco Lucchinelli's Battle of the Twins win at Laguna Seca that year. Each of the 296 bikes had a replica Marco Lucchinelli signature on its gas tank. The final limited-edition 750 F1 was the 1988 Santamonica, named after the circuit at Misano where Lucchinelli won the first round of the 1986 Formula 1 World Championship.

The entire 750 F1 line, and in particular the three limited-edition replicas, represented the end of an era for Ducati. It had started with one of the most successful Ducati racing bikes ever, the 600 TT2, and ended with a series of race replicas totally in keeping with the spirit and essence of Ducati. For many enthusiasts, these were the last true fundamentalist Ducatis.

Marco Lucchinelli won the 1986 Battle of the Twins race at Daytona on a prototype (851cc) 750 F1. Jimmy Adamo (behind) rode a similar (818cc) machine.

CHAPTER 14

851 TRICOLORE

851 Superbike Kit 1988 | 851cc liquid-cooled DOHC 90-degree twin | 92mm bore | 64mm stroke | 120hp at 10,000rpm | 364lb (165kg) | 155mph (250kmh)

When Claudio and Gianfranco Castiglioni purchased Ducati from the VM Group in 1985, they inherited an engine lineup based around the venerable Mille bevel-drive twin and the 350–750cc Pantah. Ducati's tradition since 1954 was to race, and the Castiglionis wanted this to continue. The bevel-drive engine was obsolete for racing, but the Pantah continued to achieve some success. For 1986, the Pantah was enlarged to 851cc and Marco Lucchinelli won the Battle of the Twins races at Daytona and Laguna Seca. All signs indicated that the air-cooled two-valve engine wasn't dead yet. However, the Castiglionis had other ideas. They wanted a totally modern engine that would be eligible to compete in the bourgeoning Superbike class and that would also provide a basis for future development. This new engine would need four valves per cylinder, liquid cooling, and preferably a desmodromic valve gear.

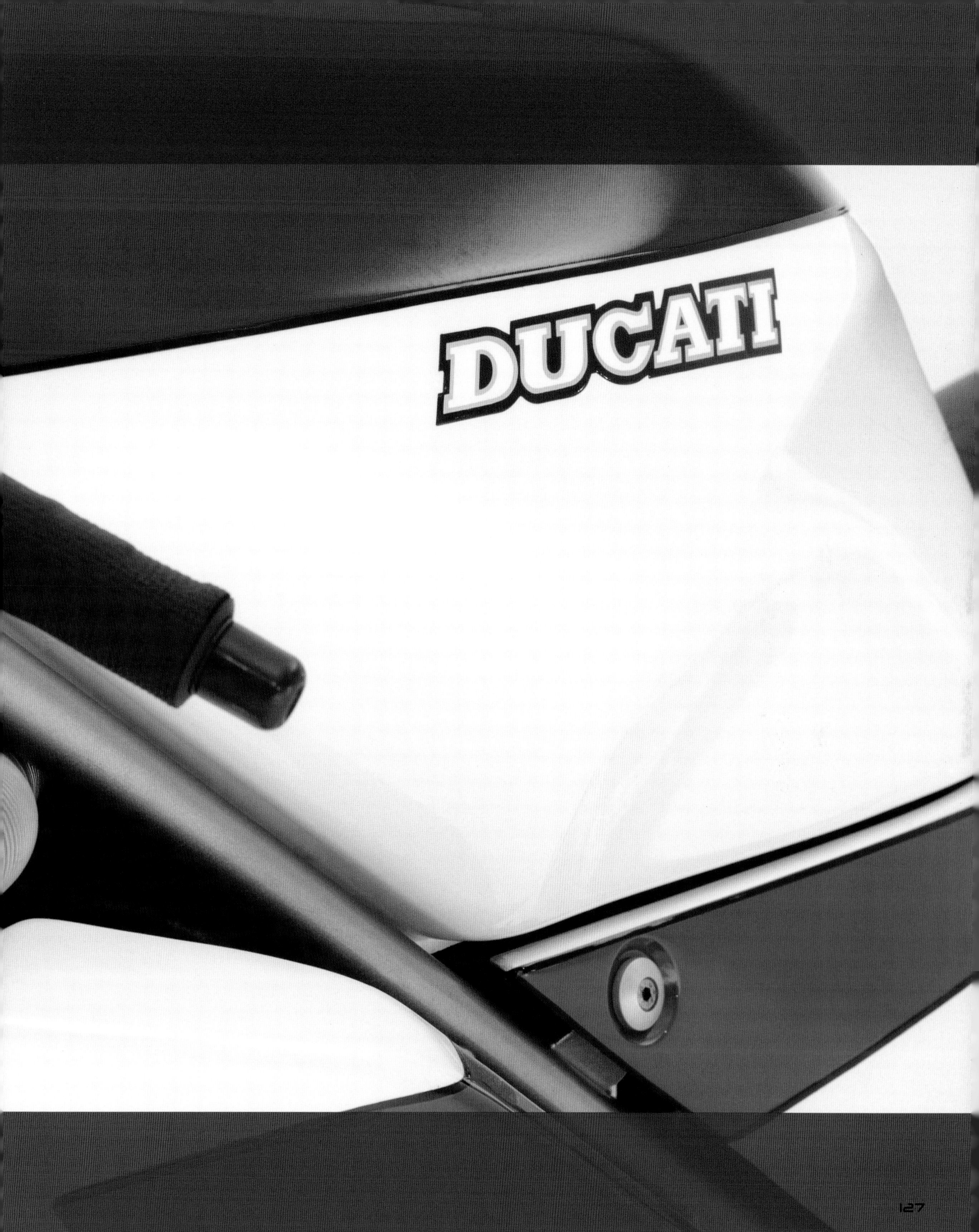
DUCATI

Show suggested that the time was right for Ducati to embrace four-valve technology. Ing. Fabio Taglioni, the designer of every successful Ducati racing engine to date, was in semi-retirement, so Cagiva looked to Ing. Massimo Bordi to coordinate the project. Bordi had joined Ducati in 1978, bringing with him an engineering thesis detailing an air-cooled four-valve desmodromic cylinder head.

Bordi was also an admirer of Cosworth, an English company created by Mike Costin and Keith Duckworth that produced some of the most successful Formula 1 car racing engines. Bordi turned to Cosworth when it came to the thermodynamic design of the four-valve cylinder head. The new liquid-cooled engine featured Pantah-style toothed rubber belts to drive the double overhead camshafts. Central to the design was the Weber Marelli open-loop fully mapped electronic fuel injection system, which employed an EPROM (electronically programmable read only memory) map of fuel and ignition requirements.

The prototype engine used modified Pantah crankcases and displaced 748cc so it could run in the Bol d'Or 24-Hour endurance race at France's Paul Ricard circuit in September 1986. To speed development, the engine was placed in a modified 750 F1 frame fitted with a braced aluminum swingarm and linkage rising-rate rear suspension. Marco Lucchinelli, Juan Garriga, and Virginio Ferrari teamed to race the prototype machine at the Bol d'Or. They rode the 748 to seventh place after thirteen hours, but were forced to retire with a broken connecting rod bolt.

With liquid cooling, four valves per cylinder, and electronic fuel injection, the 851 represented a significant technical departure for Ducati.

Marco Lucchinelli won the very first World Superbike race in 1988 on the 851.

The engine was enlarged to 851cc with a goal of winning the 1987 Daytona Battle of the Twins race. New crankcases allowed for a six-speed gearbox. The addition of twin injectors per cylinder with 47-millimeter throttle bodies saw output rise to 120 horsepower at 11,500 rpm, an astonishing figure for a twin-cylinder engine at the time. Lucchinelli easily won the race, but more significantly he was timed at 165.44 miles per hour.

The World Superbike Championship was established in 1988 and appeared tailor-made for the new 851 as twins were granted a 250cc displacement advantage and a minimum weight of 309 pounds (140 kilograms) compared to the fours' 364-pound (165-kilogram) limit. Homologation requirements for World Superbike required that Ducati build 200 units of the 851 for 1988. This homologation machine was known as the 851 Superbike Kit and was a confused mixture of racer and street bike. Here was a machine designed for racing that came with Michelin racing slicks but also included an electric starter, headlight, and taillight. Fortunately there were no turn signal indicators or rearview mirrors. Ducati produced 207 "Tricolore" (a reference to its distinctive red, white, and green color scheme) Superbike Kits, just enough to homologate the factory racer.

The heart of the Superbike kit was a race-kitted 851cc engine. Racing components included Pankl connecting rods and a closer-ratio six-speed "kit" gearbox. The Weber Marelli electronic ignition and fuel injection system was the same system as on the factory racer. The chassis of the 851 Superbike Kit reflected developments from the official 1987 racing program. The Marzocchi suspension consisted of 41.7-millimeter M1R forks and a rising-rate linkage Supermono rear shock absorber acting on a braced aluminum swingarm. Marvic 17-inch magnesium racing wheels featured state-of-the-art rim widths

(3.50 and 5.50 inches) but were fitted with only small diameter (280-millimeter) cast-iron discs at the front clamped by four-piston Brembo racing calipers.

The 851 Superbike Kit looked impressive on paper, but its main problem was excessive weight. The claim of its 364-pound (165-kilogram) weight was undoubtedly spurious. Its actual weight was closer to 419 pounds (190 kilograms), far too heavy for a racer. The weight, combined with limited information on the injection system and replacement EPROMs, made the Superbike Kit disappointing for anyone expecting to race as a privateer in Superbike. If a racer had factory assistance, however, it was a different story. Stefano Carrachi took a factory 851 Superbike Kit to Daytona in 1988, where he finished second in the Pro-Twins race. The machine then went to US-based tuner Eraldo Ferracci, who developed it further. Racer Dale Quarterley rode the Ferracci machine to the US Pro-Twins title.

Marco Lucchinelli rode the 851 to overall victory at the first World Superbike race at Donington in April 1988. Unfortunately, continual electrical and crankshaft problems caused the 851 to retire from many subsequent races. Lucchinelli finished fifth overall in that inaugural season. For 1989, the factory bike grew to 888cc, and French racer Raymond Roche took over the position as lead rider. Mechanical and electrical problems plagued the revised machine, and though Roche won more races than his competitors (five), he ended third in the championship. Ducati needed to improve the Desmoquattro's reliability, and that would happen in the next decade.

CHAPTER 15

851 SP3

1991 | 851cc Liquid-cooled DOHC 90-degree twin | 94mm bore | 64mm stroke | 128hp at 10,500rpm | 414lb (188kg) | 160mph (257kmh)

After 1989's impressive showing in the World Superbike Championship, it was inevitable that Raymond Roche and the Ducati 888 would be a major force during 1990. Not only was the 888 as fast, if not faster, than the four-cylinder competition, but its weight advantage would soon prove key. Output was increased to 130 horsepower at 11,000 rpm, but most development centered on improving reliability. The earlier electronic problems had been resolved, but now the lubrication system and crankcases were the primary areas of weakness. The chassis was much as before, though now with Öhlins suspension. The 888 began the season at 346 pounds (157 kilograms), and the weight was gradually reduced to 324 pounds (147 kilograms). Roche dominated the 1990 season, and with eight victories he provided Ducati with its first World Superbike Championship.

Superbike

851

Ducati still had to meet homologation requirements for World Superbike for 1989, so it built a small series of 851 Sport Production bikes, primarily for the Italian Sport Production series. The series pitted production 750cc fours against twins of up to 1,000cc. The 1989 851 SP was virtually indistinguishable from the production 851 Strada. Unlike the 888cc factory racers, the capacity remained at 851cc. Due to its unremarkable specification, this first-series 851 Sport Production wasn't as successful as expected. As a result, it morphed into the much higher performing 851 Sport Production 2 for 1990.

Though still titled an 851, the 851 SP2 now displaced 888cc thanks to larger (94-millimeter) pistons. There was a return to twin injectors per cylinder, and, unlike the production 851 Strada, the SP retained the H-section Pankl rods. Other upgrades included a closer ratio gearbox with revised ratios for third, fourth, fifth, and sixth gears. A 10.7:1 compression ratio and a 45-millimeter Termignoni exhaust system helped push the rear-wheel horsepower to 109 at 10,000–10,500 rpm.

Chassis improvements included an upside-down 42-millimeter Öhlins fork as used on the factory racer, an Öhlins shock absorber, and fully floating 320-millimeter Brembo cast-iron front disc brakes with higher specification Brembo calipers. The SP2 was Monoposto only and the rear subframe was aluminum; however, the heavier fork, which pushed the bike's weight to 414 pounds (188 kilograms), offset the weight savings. Only 380 851 SP2s were produced, and the model provided unparalleled handling and performance in 1990.

Each year required a new model for World Superbike homologation, and for 1991 the SP2 evolved into the similar 851 SP3. Still 888cc, the most identifiable difference from the SP2 was the louder and more upswept Termignoni exhaust system, which was a homologation exhaust for the factory racers. Larger valves (33 and 29 millimeters), higher compression (11:1) pistons, and a forced air intake all helped drive a small power increase. Experience gained from the 1990 World Superbike season resulted in stronger crankcases and a new 18-plate clutch.

The 851 SP3 continued with the same Öhlins fork, but a slightly different Öhlins shock absorber was fitted, as was a new World Superbike–homologated carbon-fiber front fender. In all other respects, the 851 SP3 was identical to the SP2. A numbered plaque was affixed to each of the 534 manufactured. Sixteen 851 Sport Production Specials also were produced for 1991, these having an even higher performance engine (Corsa specification) and more carbon-fiber components.

For the 1991 World Superbike Championship, Ducati concentrated on improving reliability and reducing the weight of its 888cc racers. Weight for the factory 888 was pared to only 315 pounds (143 kilograms), further accentuating the weight difference between twins and fours. Engine development focused on new reinforced crankcases, and the 888cc engine's power was only marginally increased: 133 horsepower at 11,500 rpm. New bodywork—including a new front fender, higher mounted silencers, and a rear fender running underneath the swingarm—developed in the Pininfarina wind tunnel improved aerodynamics by 5 percent. Another benefit from the altered position of various components was an improvement in weight distribution to 51/49 percent.

Giancarlo Falappa raced the factory 888 during 1992. This bike was still based on the earlier SP3.

Doug Polen received a factory 888 for 1991, and Ducati was well placed to repeat the 1990 result in the World Superbike Championship. But no one expected the dominance shown by Polen on the Fast by Ferracci machine. The American racer won 17 of the 26 races that season. Ducati failed to meet the World Superbike homologation target date for 1992, and the 851 SP3 continued as the homologation special for one more year. So while the new series of 888 SP4 and SPS were released as 1992 production spearheads, the factory racers for 1992 looked very similar to those in 1991. Yet while the 1992 factory racers looked a year out of date, there was nothing out of date about their performance.

After winning the World Superbike Championship in 1991 on the Fast by Ferracci Ducati 888, Doug Polen was elevated to the official factory team for 1992. The power of the 888cc engine increased marginally to 135 horsepower at 11,200 rpm, with the emphasis on a smoother power delivery. The factory machines ran an updated 42-millimeter Öhlins front fork, and further attention to weight saving and distribution saw the 888 down to the minimum 309 pounds (140 kilograms) with 52/48 percent front-to-rear weight distribution.

Polen again proved dominant, ultimately taking the title again and winning 9 of the 26 races. But increasing competition from Yamaha and Kawasaki meant 1992 would be the last year the 888 would win the World Superbike Championship.

Texan Doug Polen completely dominated the 1991 World Superbike Championship on the Fast by Ferracci 888.

CHAPTER 16

888 SPS

1992 | 888cc liquid-cooled DOHC 90-degree twin | 94mm bore | 64mm stroke | 120hp at 10,500rpm | 408lb (185kg) | over 162mph (260kmh)

The 851 was beginning to look a bit dated by 1992, but its replacement, Massimo Tamburini's new 916, was not yet ready. Pierre Terblanche was asked to provide the 851 an interim facelift with a more up-to-date appearance. This 851 update was Terblanche's first solo project for Cagiva, and he completed it within three to four weeks. This facelift, now titled an 888 (rather than 851 as in 1991), was shared with the 1992 Sport Production series, and there were two 888 Sport Production models: the SP4 and SPS (Sport Production Special). Both had a solo seat, and while the SP4 retained the specifications of the earlier SP3, the SPS provided higher performance.

The engine for the 888 SP4 had a revised cooling system and curved radiator, a new front-feed airbox, and a slightly higher compression ratio (11.2:1) but was unchanged from the SP3. The SPS engine was higher specification than the SP4's, sharing much with the customer 888 Corsa—including larger valves (34 and 30 millimeters), the inlet camshaft from the Corsa, and higher compression pistons (11.7:1).

Otherwise the 888 SPS engine was ostensibly that of the 1991 customer racing Corsa. The crankshaft carried lighter Pankl connecting rods that incorporated an additional oil way to the little end to improve under-piston cooling. The SPS also featured the Corsa's twin-injector Weber Marelli EFI, along with a Termignoni racing exhaust with carbon fiber mufflers. The cooling system was also from the Corsa, with a lightweight curved radiator and no electric fan. The SPS also received a cutaway and vented racing aluminum clutch cover. The SPS engine was very much a racing unit, not totally suited to street use.

The 888 SP4 and SPS both included the new frame of the 1992 851 Strada, with revised footpeg mounts and bent outer tubes. The rear subframe was aluminum as on the SP3, and suspension was the same Öhlins upside-down fork and shock absorber. The only difference to the braking system from the SP3 was new Brembo "Gold Series" P4.30/34 brake calipers.

From the 1992 851 Strada came the restyled pivoting gas tank, improving accessibility to the throttle and injection assembly. The tank was steel (rather than the SP3's aluminum) on the 888 SP4 while the 888 SPS had a quick-release carbon fiber tank with a carbon-fiber cap. A numbered plaque sat atop the top triple clamp on both 888 SPs (sharing the same sequence). Five hundred SP4s were manufactured, but the 888 SPS was a very limited-production machine with only 101 produced. It was undeniably the most exotic production street motorcycle available in 1992, providing performance that is still impressive more than two decades later.

The final 888 Sport Production was the 888 SP5 of 1993. With the higher performance SPS engine (but with an SP4 cooling system and 118 horsepower at 10,500 rpm), this continued to set the performance standard for twin-cylinder motorcycles. The SP5 retained all the usual SPS features, but a Showa fork replaced the expensive Öhlins unit. The SP5 couldn't meet US Department of Transportation requirements despite being noticeably more civilized than the raucous 888 SPS. Consequently, a specific US-market 888 SPO (Sport Production Omologato) was produced to homologate the bike for AMA Superbike racing. This was an amalgam of SP5 and the European-specification 888 Strada, and although titled a Sport Production, they were more closely related to the 888 Strada than to the SP5.

The 888 Corsa (customer racer) for 1992 was still based on the 1991 SP3; it wasn't until 1993 that the Corsa featured the updated styling and new frame of the 1992 888 SPS. The factory World Superbike racers also featured the updated frame and styling for 1993. Because Honda delayed the release of its new fuel-injected RC45 until the 1994 season, Ducati decided to hold the

888 SP4

DUCATI

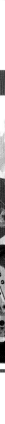

release of the 916 for another year. The venerable 888 soldiered on, now in its
seventh year of competition but still the machine to beat.

Reigning champion Doug Polen headed back to the United States to compete
in the AMA Superbike Championship, so Carl Fogarty joined Giancarlo Falappa
in the factory team. The engine started out with only a few improvements over
the 1992 title winner, but the speed of Scott Russell's Kawasaki prompted the
release of a 96x64-millimeter (926cc) engine for faster circuits. This pushed
power up to around 144 horsepower at 11,500 rpm.

The factory racers benefited from the slightly improved aerodynamics of
the new SP4 bodywork, and some components were stronger and heavier, as
the weight regulations now required twins to weigh at least 320 pounds (145
kilograms). The factory 888 remained a force to be reckoned with, and Ducati
won the constructor's championship with 19 race wins (11 of these Fogarty).
Kawasaki's Scott Russell took the rider's title, however.

Across the Atlantic, Doug Polen provided Ducati its first AMA Superbike
National Championship, winning 6 of the 10 rounds. For 1994, the factory pensioned
the 888 in favor of the new 916, but in the AMA Championship Australian Troy
Corser gave the older machine one final series championship victory.

Although there were subsequent 916 and 996 Sport Production series, the
888 SPs, and in particular the 888 SPS, represented the end of an era for Ducati.
They were built in fewer numbers than later SPs and were loud, hard-edged
race replicas offering unequaled performance for the day. Uncompromising,
raw, and brutal, they remain unique in Ducati's race lineage.

PART 4
THOROUGHLY MODERN

CHAPTER 17

SUPERMONO

1995 | 572cc liquid-cooled DOHC single | 102mm bore | 70mm stroke | 81hp at 10,000rpm | 269lb (122kg) | 149mph (240kmh)

Over Ducati's history, there have been many unfulfilled promises, but none more squandered than the Supermono. Ducati's tradition was founded on single-cylinder motorcycles, and when the Supermono was conceived, it promised to resurrect the concept, forming the foundation of a new family of high-technology single-cylinder machines. Massimo Bordi, Ducati's then engineering chief, envisaged the Supermono as the perfect single-cylinder motorcycle for both the racetrack and street. Although the Supermono project began after the 916, the Supermono prototype was unveiled a year earlier at the Cologne show at the end of 1992. It caused a sensation, and it remains one of the most beautiful and timeless of all Ducati designs. The Supermono was a catalog racer produced by the racing department and intended for "Sound of Singles" racing, much the same as the 888 Racing.

The heart of the Supermono was the engine, and development of this began during 1990. Bordi elected to adapt the 90-degree V-twin so that vibration, the traditional bugbear of big singles, could be eliminated. Bordi's original idea called for a V-twin with a dummy piston, but due to internal friction and crankcase pressure, the 487cc engine produced a disappointing 53 horsepower on its first dyno run. An increase to 57 horsepower was also deemed insufficient. Bordi then incorporated a unique counterbalancing system, attaching a second connecting rod to a lever pivoting on a pin fixed in the crankcase. Called the *doppia bielletta* (double con-rod), it was the first time this system had been used in a gas engine, although it had previously featured on diesel engines. Bordi had considerable experience with small, direct-injection diesels because he was involved with VM diesel development at Ducati from 1978 until he started working on motorcycle engines in 1982.

The revised Supermono engine was more compact than the earlier design, and it replicated the twin's perfect primary balance without the burden of friction. Power rose immediately to 62.5 horsepower at 10,500 rpm. The next development stage saw a 502cc version (95.6x70 millimeters) that produced 70 horsepower. The development team, led by Gianluigi Mengoli and Claudio Domenicali, then created a larger cylinder with a wider stud pattern. This allowed a 100-millimeter cylinder and a British Omega 11.8:1 piston. This 549cc version produced 75 horsepower at 10,000 rpm and went into limited production during 1993. Even at 10,000 rpm, the large single was as smooth as a twin. It was a brilliant concept, both in design and execution.

Many of the Supermono's features were inherited from the 888 Racing, including liquid-cooling, the double overhead camshaft four-valve desmodromic cylinder head, and an identical Weber I.A.W. Alfa/N fuel injection system with twin injectors. Throttle body diameter tapered from 50 millimeters to 47 millimeters at the butterfly. The valve sizes were 37 and 31 millimeters, and the camshafts used the same profile as the 926cc 1994 888 Racing. There were some important departures in the engine design, notably the use of much stronger 49-millimeter plain main bearings, a dry 180-watt alternator, and the water pump driven off the exhaust camshaft. Many other engine components were specific to the Supermono, including the crankcases, cylinders, crankshaft, and gearbox. As with the 888 Racing, the two connecting rods were titanium Pankl. The 50-millimeter exhaust exited on the right into either a Termignoni single or dual-outlet muffler.

Housing this remarkable engine was a TIG-welded tubular steel frame built by Cagiva Telai in Varese, with an aluminum Verlicchi-made swingarm. Each frame was individually crafted and intended only for limited production. The 916 frame appeared crude by comparison. The Supermono's rear suspension was by cantilever, but with a 9 percent rising rate due to the mounting angle. Only the highest quality suspension components were fitted: a 42-millimeter Öhlins inverted fork with magnesium triple clamps up front and a ride-height adjustable Öhlins shock absorber in back.

A steering head angle of 23 degrees and a compact wheelbase of 53.5 inches (1,360 millimeters) assured responsive handling. Even more significant than the chassis dimensions was the weight distribution, which placed 54.5 percent of the bike's weight on the front wheel. Brembo brakes and 17-inch magnesium Marchesini wheels were full racing specifications.

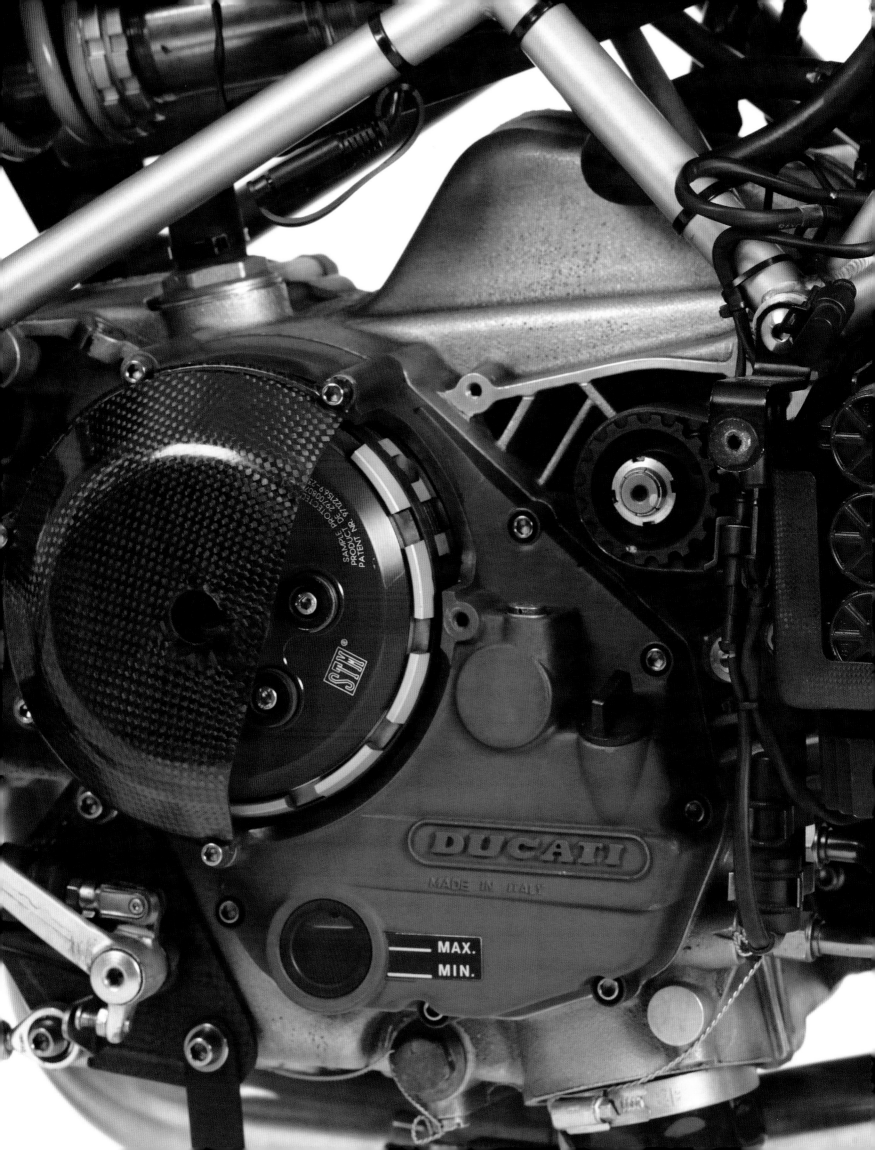

When the Supermono debuted, it wore stunning, full carbon fiber bodywork designed by Pierre Terblanche in just two months. The Supermono finally went into production during 1993 built solely as a Sounds of Singles racer by the racing department. Only 30 were manufactured that year, plus another 10 in 1994.

The Supermono suffered up to a 50 percent deficit in capacity compared to some of the specialized single-cylinder racers it competed against. In fine Ducati tradition, it relied on finesse and balance to achieve success. A larger version was created for 1995, its 102-millimeter piston yielding 572cc. Updates included a revised EPROM and silencer and a new 42-millimeter Öhlins front fork and longer shock absorber. Even this capacity increase wasn't enough to ensure racetrack dominance, and after only 25 more examples were built, that was the end of the Supermono. (A Supermono engine was placed in a 900 SS frame in 1998 with a view to implementing production, but nothing came of the exercise.)

Apart from the ability to rev smoothly to previously unheard of levels for a big single, much of the Supermono's exceptional ability was due to its remarkably low center of gravity. Perfectly balanced and proportioned, the Supermono offered everything: stability, agility, quick steering, and amazing response. It's a shame such a wonderful machine never made it to regular production.

CHAPTER 18

916 FOGARTY REPLICA

1998 | 996cc liquid-cooled DOHC 90-degree twin | 98mm bore | 66mm stroke | 123hp at 9,500rpm (crank) | 419lb (190kg) | 168mph (270kmh)

As Ducati's piecemeal approach to the development of the 888 continued, work was quietly and steadily proceeding on an evolutionary four-valve Ducati. Ducati's new owners, the Castiglionis, recognized the need for the new four-valve Ducati to be a total engineering package with fully coordinated styling. Thus, as Massimo Bordi and his team continued developing the 851, Cagiva design chief Massimo Tamburini was given the charter to create the 916.

Development encompassed six years, and the 916 would be one of Ducati's most comprehensive designs. Despite this, it maintained Ducati's tradition of evolution as Tamburini eschewed Japanese and Bimota-style aluminum delta-box frames in preference to the established space frame. Racing was seen as pivotal to the success of the 916, so the final configuration provided a 20-millimeter-shorter wheelbase (1,410 millimeters) than that of the 888, with 49 percent of the weight on the front wheel. An important element of the frame design was an additional lower engine support, contributing to increased rigidity, with the single-sided swingarm now supported by the frame in addition to the engine cases. Unique chassis features included an extremely strong steering head structure with the provision for adjustable caster without altering the wheelbase and deep, machined triple clamps. This latter modification is indicative of the attention to detail that Tamburini and his team paid to significant components. The triple clamps also provided increased rigidity and contributed to the 916's superior handling.

Another important consideration in the design was a reduction in frontal area and an improvement in aerodynamics over the 851/888. Almost every component was individually designed and crafted. Nothing exemplified the attention to detail more than the beautifully executed headlight support and the twin poly-ellipsoidal headlights. Twin taillights specifically styled for the

916 and an exhaust system designed to aid aerodynamics more than ultimate power completed the 916's unique overall design. As a complete package, the 916's groundbreaking design set a style blueprint that nearly all other manufacturers came to emulate.

The engine came in for a major redesign as well. With a goal to make a full liter engine at some point in the future, the stroke was lengthened 2 millimeters to 66 millimeters. With 94-millimeter pistons, this provided displacement of 916cc. Technically the revised engine was only an evolution of the 851, but it was executed so brilliantly that it was almost as if the 916 was a completely new model. The 916's balance between engine and chassis set new standards. There was a homogeneity about the design that took the 916 into another dimension.

The 916 also took the company beyond that of an enthusiast niche-market manufacturer to the creator of a universally admired and desirable motorcycle. The 916 was revolutionary visually, and it is one of the most beautifully balanced and aesthetically satisfying street motorcycles ever conceived. But it was only after success on the racetrack that the 916 finally assumed the status of the world's most desirable sporting motorcycle.

As with all great Ducatis, the 916 was created primarily as a racer and subsequently adapted for the street. One of the most significant advantages of the 916 over the earlier 888 was the compactness of the design and the small overall size. The 916 was surprisingly successful for a new model, both on the track and in the showroom. Carl Fogarty was hampered after breaking a wrist early in the 1994 World Superbike season, but he came back to win the

The 916's headlight treatment established a fresh design blueprint for the motorcycle industry.

championship on a 916. The factory racer displaced 955cc for the 1994 and 1995 seasons, and its improved reliability saw Fogarty dominate the 1995 series. Fogarty left Ducati for 1996, but Troy Corser stepped in to provide Ducati with another championship. The factory bike now displaced 996cc beginning in 1996, but reliability had become an issue.

Ducati continued to produce a limited number of Sport Production models for homologation, and for 1997 it produced the 916 SPS (Sport Production Special). Reliability problems with the racing 996 during 1996 mandated that a new set of stronger crankcases be homologated for the 1997 racing season. This was the 916 SPS's primary purpose. Carl Fogarty returned to the factory World Superbike team in 1997 and finished second in the World Superbike Championship behind John Kocinski's Honda.

The loss of both the riders' and constructors' titles in the 1997 World Superbike Championship prompted Ducati to expand its official program for 1998 with Carl Fogarty again riding for Team Ducati Performance. The 1998 996 was an immediate improvement over the 1997 bike, but it still lacked power, and the dominance of earlier seasons remained elusive. However, a significant development occurred for the South African round at Kyalami in early July. A newly homologated frame (via the 916 SPS Fogarty Replica profiled here) allowed the rear bracing tube to be moved back and downward, thus locating

the engine slightly lower than before. The alteration of one of the top transverse frame tubes under the fuel tank created space for a larger capacity airbox and allowed a revised air intake with shorter intakes, now completely inside the airbox. These developments improved the 996 racer dramatically. The torque curve was flatter, and there was more top-end power (reputedly 7–8 horsepower). This seemingly simple frame modification proved the single most effective development of the 996 in recent years. At the first Kyalami race, Ducatis filled the first three places. Fogarty won the 1998 World Superbike Championship and went on to win again in 1999.

The 202 Fogarty Replica 916 SPSs built to homologate the World Superbike "Kyalami" frame were available only in England. While they were nearly identical to the regular 916 SPS, there were a few extra touches to ensure exclusivity. The decals were patterned on the Ducati Performance 996 World Superbike racer of Carl Fogarty, and the wheels were black five-spoke Marchesinis rather than the regular gold three-spoke Brembos. The fuel tank, bike cover, and key fob also came with a Fogarty signature. Other features specific to the Fogarty Replica included a titanium exhaust system and a carbon-fiber seat unit with racing Tecnosel seat pad. So successful was the limited-edition Fogarty version that another series was produced for 1999 and 2000.

CHAPTER 19

MH900e

2001 | 904cc air-cooled 90-degree twin | 92mm bore | 68mm stroke | 75hp at 8,000rpm (rear wheel) | 403lb (183kg) | 140mph (225kmh)

Ducati's approach to limited-production specials changed significantly with the release of the MH900e in 2000. Prior to the MH900e, limited-edition models were mostly race replicas or homologation specials, but the MH900e differed in that it was more of a factory custom, honoring tradition rather than outright performance. Also, unlike other limited editions, the MH900e was a personal interpretation by Ducati designer Pierre Terblanche.

Terblanche had particularly fond memories of the magnificent NCR racers of the mid- to late-1970s. He had wanted to create a design inspired by these beautiful machines ever since Mike Hailwood rode one to victory at the Isle of Man in 1978. With the new-generation fuel-injected 900 Super Sport complete, Terblanche had time on his hands. Over the summer of 1998, he traveled to England and worked on the idea with A K A Design and Realization Services in Hitchin, north of London. Over an eleven-week period, he worked with a three-dimensional computer model and then constructed a full-size clay model. This extensive use of computer-aided design was a first for Ducati. The idea behind the Evoluzione was neo classical. Though inspired by Hailwood's NCR racer, it was to be simple in essence, eliminating many superfluous modern components to replicate the classic feel of the '60s and '70s. Terblanche wanted to get away from complexity and carbon fiber, emphasizing the elemental nature and breaking the motorcycle into four distinct elements: engine, frame, wheels, and bodywork.

An air-cooled, two-valve, fuel-injected 900 Super Sport engine was the starting point, tidied externally through the use of sump covers to hide the oil cooler and lines and with the ignition coils on the camshaft bearing supports on the cylinder heads. The engine had polished cases reminiscent of the early-1970s "round-case" Ducatis, but apart from the lightweight (800 grams) titanium and carbon fiber slipper clutch, it was a standard 900 Super Sport. The exhaust system recalled the megaphone style of the 1970s, with the volume increased to 12 liters to meet homologation requirements.

The tubular steel frame was a special construction by the Dutch company Troll and featured a strong 60-millimeter backbone integrated with a series of smaller-diameter steel wishbones placing the engine as far forward in the frame as possible. Though a twin shock swingarm in the style of the original Hailwood Replica was considered initially, this was discarded for a tubular single-sided swingarm with Öhlins shock absorber and modern Showa upside down fork. A single 305-millimeter disc graced the front, helping to minimize unsprung weight. The disc was made of a Russian space-age material and glowed a spectacular red when operated in the dark.

One of the more advanced features was the one-piece, nylon polymer fairing and fuel-tank unit designed to keep as much weight on the front wheel as possible. The red and silver colors represented those of the original NCR rather than the Castrol colors of Hailwood's Sport Motorcycles machine. Other details included rear turn signals incorporated in the exhaust outlets; a small, 80-millimeter diameter Valeo headlight; a voice-activated ignition system; and a television rear-view camera. The prototype MH900e was first displayed at the end of 1998, and it caused a sensation. It looked stunning, promising quality and exclusivity if it made it into production.

Ducati decided to produce only 1,000 examples of the MH900e. Because only one version was available, the company chose a bold and innovative method for commercialization: the Internet. Orders for the Đ15,000 (approximately $15,000) machine were only accepted on Ducati's Web site, with availability beginning on New Year's Day 2000. The MH900e proved so popular that initial

production estimates were revised upwards. Ducati showed that it was at the forefront of motorcycle marketing, and this sales method would be used again for future limited-edition models. Production commenced mid-2000 with first production examples delivered in June at the World Ducati Weekend at Misano. Most were built in 2001 and sold into 2002, with just over 2,000 manufactured.

The production MH900e was surprisingly faithful to the prototype. The same Marelli fuel-injected 904cc engine of the 900 Super Sport powered it, but with plastic cosmetic engine sump covers hiding some of the more unsightly components. The oil cooler was now located externally, and the clutch was a conventional dry multiplate unit rather than the exotic lightweight slipper type. The tubular steel frame, single-sided swingarm, and unique red and silver bodywork were unchanged, but the wheels, brakes, and suspension were the same as those on various production models. The twin 320-millimeter semifloating front discs with Brembo P30/34 calipers were from the 900 Super Sport, the five-spoke 17-inch Marchesini wheels came from the 996 Superbike, and the Paioli rear shock absorber was sourced from the 750 Super Sport. The nonadjustable, 43-millimeter Showa upside down fork also came from the 750 Super Sport, a rather strange choice considering the production 900 Super Sport front fork was fully adjustable. A regular 130-millimeter headlight replaced the small Valeo of the prototype, and the turn signals were no longer in the exhaust pipe outlets, but many of the individual detail components remained. These included the stainless-steel front fender and taillight mounts and milled aluminium footpegs.

Though the production version of the MH900e may have seemed a random synthesis of existing components, the execution was impeccable and the basic ingredients still provided functional superiority. Every detail ensured a bridge was created between the inspiration of the past and the reality of the present, and the MH900e's success ensured this factory custom concept would continue in the future.

The MH900e was a personal vision of its creator, Pierre Terblanche, here with the prototype at the factory in 1998.

CHAPTER 20

998 R

2002 | 999cc liquid-cooled DOHC 90-degree twin | 104mm bore | 58.8mm stroke | 139hp at 10,000rpm | 403lb (183kg) | 174mph (280kmh)+

Despite the continued success of the 996 Desmoquattro on the racetrack and in the showroom, it was obvious this venerable design couldn't last forever. Ducati was aware that time was running out for its Desmoquattro even before Honda won the 2000 World Superbike Championship. The design that first appeared in 1986 as a 748 was still responding to development, but the competition had finally caught up. It was time for a reevaluation of the L-twin desmodromic concept. Ducati and desmo were synonymous so the company opted for evolution, not revolution.

By early 1998, the formula and design parameters for a new engine, the Testastretta, were established, and an outside consultant was engaged to design the desmodromic cylinder head. The use of outside consultants wasn't new to Ducati. Ricardo in England had produced a 500cc Grand Prix three-cylinder engine in 1971 and the Bolognese engineer Renato Armaroli was responsible for the four-valve belt-drive 500cc V-twin Grand Prix engine of 1973. When it came to selecting a consultant for the Testastretta engine, Ducati turned to retired Formula 1 Ferrari engineer Ing. Angiolino Marchetti. Marchetti came with more than 30 years experience with Ferrari, and he also had experience with desmodromic valve gears. Back in the late 1980s, Marchetti was involved with Ferrari's desmodromic V-12 Formula 1 engine, complete with 96 opening and closing rockers. Marchetti worked closely with Ing. Massimo Bordi in the design of the Testastretta, but he died in 1999 without seeing the project to its conclusion.

One of the most important requirements in the design of the cylinder head was a reduction in the earlier included valve angle of 40 degrees. It wasn't difficult to design a new cylinder head with a narrower valve angle, but retaining desmodromic valve actuation with steep downdraft ports presented a challenge. Marchetti and Bordi decided on a flatter 25-degree included valve angle that, with the larger bore, permitted oversized valves while still providing a high compression ratio with a flat-topped piston. The narrower valve angle required a complete redesign of the existing Desmoquattro rocker layout. The difficulty came with the support of the closing arms inside the head while maintaining a central spark plug. Marchetti's solution was to insert a central cast steel sleeve for the spark plug, also using a single 10-millimeter spark plug instead of the previous 12-millimeter version.

As this new engine would eventually power an entire range of motorcycles, it was also important that the overall cylinder head be more compact. Thus the engine was named Testastretta, that is "narrow head." The larger bore

and shallower valve angle allowed for larger valves (40-millimeter intake and 33-millimeter exhaust) than on the 996. Another advantage of the Testastretta cylinder head design was steeper, downdraft porting to give the mixture a straighter path to the valves.

The new engine involved much more than just a new cylinder head. The search for higher revs, along with improved cylinder filling and combustion, required a shorter 63.5-millimeter stroke, which allowed revs to climb beyond 13,000 rpm. With a 100-millimeter bore, the new engine displaced 998cc.

For the first time since 1988, the crankcases were redesigned. They remained vertically split, but the cylinders were rotated 10 degrees backward to assist gravity oil scavenging from the front cylinder. The crankcases also included a *coppa bossa*, or bottom cup, an oil sump extension that incorporated the oil pump pickup. Also new was the Magneti Marelli 5.9M electronic ignition and injection control unit with 54-millimeter throttle bodies and elliptical chokes.

Though the Testastretta was to be the engine spearheading Ducati's performance lineup for the near future, full-scale production couldn't be implemented initially. For 2001, the 998cc Testastretta engine was placed in the existing 996 chassis, thus creating the limited-edition 996 R, the World Superbike homologation special. Troy Bayliss proved the Testastretta racing engine's potential by winning the 2001 World Superbike Championship.

For 2002, the 998cc Testastretta engine made it into regular production as the 998, and the 996 R evolved into the 998 R. The model designation didn't reflect the actual capacity, as the 998 R Testastretta featured an even larger bore and shorter stroke. With a compression ratio of 12.3:1, the 998 R was the most powerful Ducati street bike ever produced.

In most other respects, the 998 R was similar to the earlier 996 R, sharing the same modified Fogarty-type chrome-molybdenum frame, TiN-coated Öhlins fork, and Öhlins shock absorber. Differences included five-spoke Marchesini wheels that were lighter than those on the 996 R, by 400 grams (14 ounces) on the front and 800 grams (28 ounces) on the rear, and the brake discs were more offset to improve cooling. The carbon fiber fairing was joined by a carbon fiber tailpiece to further reduce weight.

The short-stroke Testastretta promised much, but still Bayliss narrowly lost the 2002 World Superbike Championship to Honda's Colin Edwards. For 2003, the 998 would be replaced by Terblanche's new-generation 999. The 999 R promised superior all-round performance, though for some the 998 R still reigned supreme. As the final example of the 916-derived limited-edition homologation models, the 998 R is arguably the finest.

CHAPTER 21

999 R XEROX

2006 | 999cc liquid-cooled DOHC 90-degree twin | 104mm bore | 58.8mm stroke | 150hp at 9,750rpm | 399lb (181kg) | 180mph (290kmh)+

The loss of the 2002 World Superbike Championship proved that even a brilliant design like Tamburini's 916 couldn't stay on top forever. Terblanche's 2003 replacement, the 999, took a different route, emphasizing simplicity and ergonomics. The new machine was purposefully long, low, and narrow, to reduce frontal area while still retaining many of Ducati's trademark features. Design briefs called for lowering the seat height 15 millimeters, lengthening the swingarm 15 millimeters, and reducing the seat-to-handlebar distance to 10 millimeters. For the first time, a Ducati sport bike was ergonomically designed with the rider considered as an integral component. The ergonomic brief included five-way adjustable footrests and on Monoposto versions a seat/tank unit that slid fore and aft 20 millimeters to adjust to rider height. Simplification and ease of maintenance were also primary considerations, and the 999 featured 230 (30 percent) fewer parts than the 916 it replaced.

Ostensibly the 139-horsepower 999 R Testastretta engine was carried over from the 998 R. In reality, there were a number of detail changes. Both the intake and exhaust system were redesigned. The exhaust system and single-muffler were asymmetrical, the varying pipe diameter designed to simulate equal-length exhausts. The airbox expanded to 12.5 liters with a Helmotz resonator reducing intake noise without sacrificing performance. A major innovation was the incorporation of a CAN (controller area network) line electrical system consisting of only two wires with two connected nodes: the instrument panel and the Magneti Marelli 5.9M engine control unit. This limited the number of electrical cable bundles and eliminated sensor duplication. The information from each sensor was sent to the closest processing unit, which then transmitted the information to the network and the CPUs. Overall the electrical system was simpler and lighter than on the 998.

Terblanche retained Ducati's signature steel trellis frame but fit a new double-sided, sand-cast aluminum swingarm designed to ensure optimum stiffness without increasing weight. Two horizontal sliders allowed chain tension adjustment without changing the ride height. One goal with the redesigned chassis was to place more weight on the front wheel. Just as on the 998, front fork rake was adjustable via an eccentric in the steering head. This adjustment did not alter the 55.9-inch (1,420-millimeter) wheelbase. The 999 R chassis was suspended by an Öhlins 43-millimeter front fork and rear shock. Racing-style Brembo radial front brake calipers were included for the first time on a production Ducati.

The 999's styling offered a significant departure from the 998's, particularly at the front where the narrow fairing featured a pair of vertically stacked poly-ellipsoidal headlamps. Other features included innovative mid and lower air conveyors and turbulence-reducing forward air vents. At the rear of the bike, the muffler doubled as an active aerodynamic component.

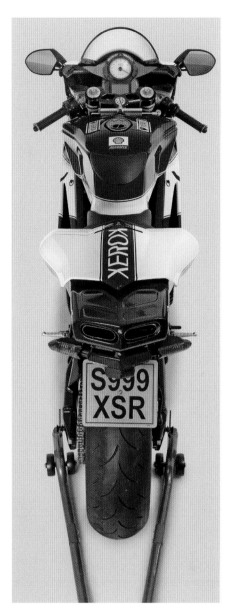

James Toseland won the 2004 World Superbike Championship on the 999 and carried the #1 plate during 2005.

The 999 was an improvement over the 998 SS, evidenced by Neil Hodgson's 2003 World Superbike championship. The attention to weight distribution, the lower center of gravity, and the longer swingarm and wheelbase contributed to a machine with improved stability under braking and acceleration.

During 2003, a limited-edition 999 R Fila was released. Celebrating 200 World Superbike victories, this was produced in the livery of Team Ducati Fila. Updates over the standard 999 R included racing-type forged wheels, a titanium headlight assembly, a carbon-fiber fairing, and a racing exhaust with a matching remapped CPU.

James Toseland followed Hodgson to win the 2004 World Superbike Championship. Clearly the 999 was very successful, but for 2005 it was significantly updated. This was driven by Ducati's return to the US AMA Superbike Championship. Updates for 2005 included restyling of the bodywork and a series of chassis and engine improvements. The engine for the 2005 999 R was uprated significantly over the previous version and incorporated many features from the racing engines, making it the most powerful production Ducati ever. The deep-sump crankcases were sandcast, and the cylinder heads were redesigned with larger squish areas and modified exhaust ports. The cylinder head included new, higher lift camshafts and larger diameter (42-millimeter and 34-millimeter) thin-stemmed titanium valves. The valve shim retaining

system was identical to the racing 999, as were the stiffer connecting rods and crankshaft. Scoops drawing air from the front of the fairing cooled the timing belt covers, the airbox was larger, and the Marelli injection system featured 12Ðhole injectors and a more sophisticated ECU.

Chassis improvements for 2005 included a new box-section swingarm with a reinforcement plate underside on the left. This reduced weight 500 grams while improving torsional rigidity 27 percent. The Y-shaped Brembo/Marchesini aluminum wheels were now forged (rather than cast), saving 7 pounds (3.2 kilograms), and a new 43-millimeter Öhlins fork was featured. The 999 fairing was also changed to more closely resemble the factory racing machines. Both the top and bottom fairing sections were redesigned to improve aerodynamics; the cockpit was larger and more rounded, with no upper airflow ducts; and a higher Plexiglas screen was fitted. The lower fairing was now more streamlined, and the lateral airflow deflectors were more rounded in profile and more enveloping. The entire fairing was constructed of carbon fiber on the 999 R. The number of footrest positions on the 2005 999 R reduced from five to two to comply with World Superbike regulations and allow for a larger diameter exhaust system.

When Troy Bayliss returned to the World Superbike team for 2006, Ducati released a celebratory Xerox edition 999 R. In addition to special graphics, the Xerox edition had a black anodized steering head and footrests, a racing-type Öhlins rear shock absorber, and a red Brembo Racing logo on the radial calipers and their mounts. Bayliss went on to win the 2006 World Superbike Championship.

The 999 R was scheduled for imminent replacement, but in this final incarnation, it was a fantastic machine and is still underappreciated for its excellence.

The 2006 factory racing 999 Testastretta engine shared many components with the 999 R Xerox.

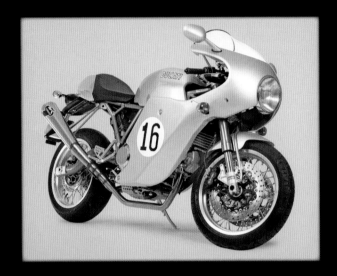

CHAPTER 22

PAUL SMART 1000 LIMITED EDITION

2006 | 992cc air-cooled 90-degree twin | 94mm bore | 71.5mm stroke | 92hp at 8,000rpm | 399lb (181kg) | 137mph (220kmh)

Toward the end of 2003, Ducati previewed three new concept bikes at the Tokyo Motor Show. Pierre Terblanche created these to embody the style and sporting heritage of the classic 1970s trio of "round-case" 750s. The response was so overwhelmingly positive to the SportClassics, as they were called, that two years later they went into production. The SportClassic line was headed by the Paul Smart 1000 Limited Edition, a modern interpretation of the iconic "green-frame" 750 Super Sport. Completing the SportClassic lineup was the Sport 1000 (inspired by the yellow 750 Sport) and the GT 1000 that harked back to the 750 GT.

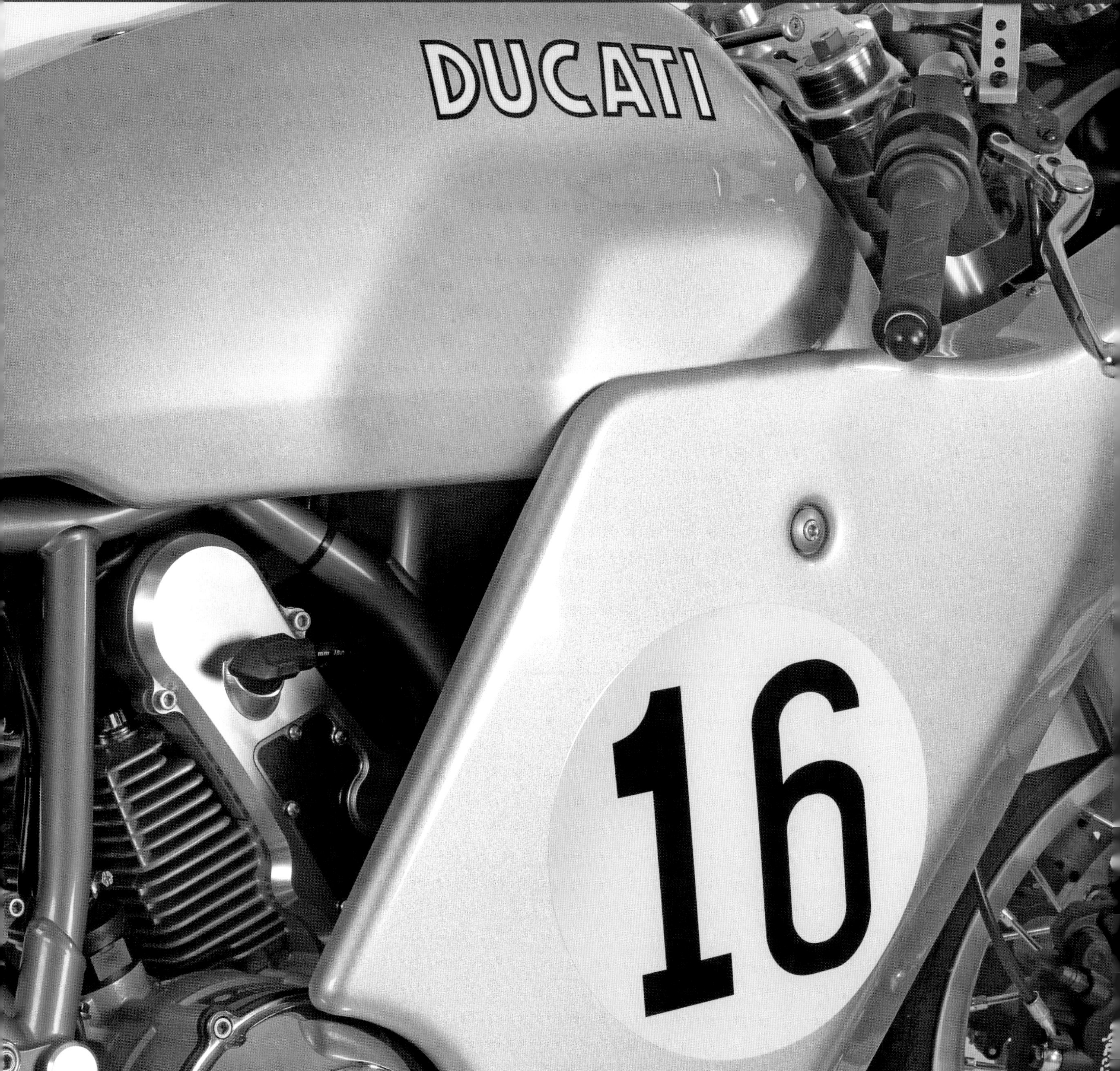
DUCATI
16

The 1974 Ducati 750 Super Sport was long and low, with a minimalist racing style, curving lines, an exposed engine, and a distinctive frame color. It was conceived as a replica of the desmodromic 750 ridden to victory in the 1972 Imola 200 race by English rider Paul Smart. Designer Pierre Terblanche sought to emulate this style using an air-cooled 1000DS engine, exposed tubular steel frame, twin rear shocks, and traditional wire-spoke wheels complemented by elegant rounded bodywork. The idea was to reflect the finest attributes of the past but incorporate modern technology and engineering. Thus the SportClassic wasn't a true race replica in the vein of the original 750 Super Sport, but more of a modern stylistic rendition of a classic theme. Instead of paying homage to the bike that won the Imola 200, as he did with his earlier Mike Hailwood Evoluzione, Terblanche in this case honored the rider, Paul Smart.

Powering the Paul Smart 1000 was the Dual Spark engine initially developed for the 2002 Multistrada. Gianluigi Mengoli's Research and Development Department updated the long-serving, two-valve, air-cooled engine with new cylinder heads, featuring a narrower included valve angle of 56 degrees, additional cooling fins, and twin spark plugs per cylinder. The valves were also larger (45 and 40 millimeters), with thinner stems (7 millimeters), and the timing pulley diameter was increased to allow the belt to follow a more direct route.

Mengoli's group also redesigned the crankshaft with more centralized mass and repositioned oil delivery ports fed by an improved lubrication system. The clutch basket and driven plates were aluminum, and the transmission output shaft was now supported by a double-row bearing on the drive side. The DS displaced 992cc, making it Ducati's largest capacity air-cooled twin since the Mille some 20 years earlier. A Magneti Marelli electronic control unit sat under the rear of the seat and featured a reprogrammable Flash EPROM. Custom features specific to the PS 1000 included chrome-plated clutch and timing inspection covers and polished valve covers.

The SportClassic models all received a new tubular steel trellis frame, the PS 1000's painted the sea green of the 1974 750 Super Sport. The 2003 prototype featured a blue frame to match Paul Smart's Imola racer, but the eventual production version reverted to the paint scheme of the production 750 Super Sport. The design department was unaware that back in 1972 Paul Smart had repainted the racing bike frame with the only match he could find at the time, that of a Hillman Imp.

Also unique to the Paul Smart (and Sport) was the welded tubular steel tube swingarm. This featured a GP-style elliptical right arm to accommodate the new exhaust system with stacked twin silencers, with a crossmember and arched tube joining the elliptical arm with the round one (on the chain side), at the single rear shock absorber mount. The two swingarm legs were made of extruded, bent tubing, with the crossmember created by hydroforming. The chain tensioning system was also reminiscent of the Seeley-type adjusters of the original 750s but was considerably more robust.

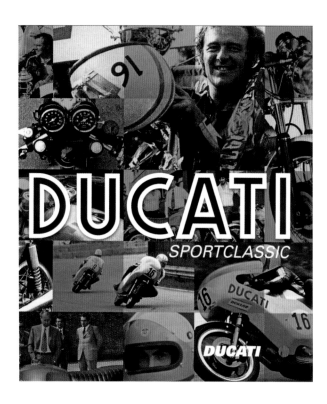

A fully adjustable Öhlins suspension (including a 43-millimeter fork) and traditional wire-spoke hubs laced to 17-inch Excel aluminum rims completed the chassis specification. In an effort to provide modern handling with a traditional look, each wheel had 36 chrome-plated spokes, with a variable taper from 5 millimeters at the hub to 4.4 millimeters at the rim. The wheels featured center-spoke drilled rims, which required tube tires, in this case wearing the same pattern as Pirelli Phantoms from the early 1980s. The spoked wheels required a more compact brake caliper, so front brake duties were handled by Brembo with thermally insulated 30- and 32-millimeter pistons. The semifloating front discs were 320 millimeters, while the rear brake was a floating single-piston Brembo brake caliper and a 245-millimeter disc. The exhaust system was a distinctive black chrome and stainless steel, with stacked mufflers on the right. Other retro features included the rounded taillight and chromed turn signals and the battery housing with drilled base. Further high-quality touches included a polished Sachs steering damper with chrome-plated rod.

Compared to the original 750 Super Sport, the Paul Smart 1000 provided considerably more modern handling. The 56-inch (1,425-millimeter) wheelbase was slightly longer than other Ducati Sport bikes but far shorter than the 59-inch (1,500-millimeter) wheelbase of the 1974 bike. The 24-degree fork rake provided quick steering, and with modern wheels sizes and suspension, the overall performance and handling was in another league from the original. Only 2,000 Paul Smart 1000 Limited Editions were produced, and they were not only a highly successful contemporary interpretation of the iconic 750 Super Sport, but a fitting tribute to Paul Smart, a rider who provided Ducati one of its greatest victories.

PART 5

SUPERIORITY THROUGH TECHNOLOGY

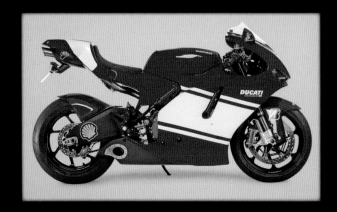

CHAPTER 23

DESMOSEDICI RR

2008 | 989cc liquid-cooled DOHC 90-degree V-four | 112mm bore | 60.8mm stroke | 200hp at 13,800rpm | 377lb (171kg) wet | 186mph (300kmh)

After more than a decade dominating the World Superbike Championship for production-based motorcycles, Ducati announced in 2002 that it would compete in MotoGP, the world's premier motorcycle racing class. MotoGP switched from 500cc two-strokes to 990cc four-strokes in 2002, and as a four-stroke manufacturer Ducati accepted the challenge of taking on the world's best in the top class. Previous attempts at Grand Prix racing in the 500cc class had proven fruitless. In the early 1970s, Ducati simply didn't have the resources to match Giacomo Agostini on the 500cc MV Agusta, and the two-stroke onslaught beginning in 1975 ended all hope of a four-stroke resurrection. But with a clean sheet of paper in a four-stroke series, Ducati believed it could mount a serious challenge. In Ducati's very first race, the 2003 Japanese Grand Prix, Loris Capirossi finished third, with Troy Bayliss fifth. In only its sixth race, in Catalunya, Capirossi provided the Desmosedici its first victory. Ducati's faith was vindicated and the skeptics answered.

DUCATI
DESMOSEDICI RR

DUCATI

ÖHLINS

brembo

Tradition was central to the philosophy of the MotoGP project. The new racers employed Fabio Taglioni's trademark desmodromic valve system, the L-cylinder layout, and the steel trellis chassis using the engine as an integral component. Filippo Preziosi headed Ducati's group of young technicians. They initially considered taking advantage of regulations that provided twin-cylinder machines a considerable weight advantage. But detailed analysis revealed a twin would have to rev beyond 17,000 rpm to produce competitive power, thus requiring an extremely short stroke and large bore. Such a combination presented combustion problems, so Ducati opted for a new V-4 engine, still in the traditional 90-degree L-twin layout and retaining desmodromic valve control. This marriage of tradition and innovation proved a successful path, and the engine was titled Desmosedici (Desmosixteen). As on the L-twin, the 90-degree cylinder layout provided the perfect primary balance, allowing the engine to rev to 17,000 rpm with minimal vibration.

Ducati Corse produced two versions of the Desmosedici engine initially, one with a regular firing order, and the other with paired cylinders firing simultaneously (Twin-Pulse). As the latter version put some engine components through excessive strain, the regular firing configuration was used during 2003. Subsequent development saw the irregular firing Twin-Pulse version provide improved drivability, so this firing scheme was used during 2004. While all other manufacturers raced with varying versions of an aluminum Deltabox frame, the Desmosedici retained a tubular steel trellis structure similar to that of the World Superbike 998 and 999.

The Desmosedici RR was remarkably similar to the factory racing GP6.

Ducati's on-track success grew. Capirossi won another three Grands Prix in 2006, finishing the season third overall. After dominating the 2006 World Superbike Championship on the 999 F06, Troy Bayliss accepted a wildcard ride on the Desmosedici and won the final MotoGP race of 2006.

MotoGP regulations changed in 2007, with 800cc four-strokes replacing the 990cc bikes. Thus 2007 was an opportune time for Ducati to release the Desmosedici RR, a MotoGP 2006 (GP6) replica, the only MotoGP replica ever put into production and offered for general sale. The year 2007 was also a benchmark one for Ducati, as Casey Stoner provided Ducati with its first MotoGP World Championship.

Powering the Desmosedici RR was an engine amazingly similar to the 989cc GP6's. This included the asymmetrical Twin-Pulse configuration (with the crankpins offset 70 degrees), sand-cast aluminum crankcase and cylinder heads, four titanium desmodromic valves per cylinder, double overhead camshafts driven by a train of straight-cut gears, titanium connecting rods, a six-speed racing cassette-type transmission, a hydraulically actuated dry multiplate slipper clutch, and sand-cast magnesium engine covers.

Engine management was also similar to the GP6's: four 50-millimeter Magneti Marelli throttles with 12-hole microjet injectors and a Magneti Marelli ECU with high-speed CAN line electronics. The standard exhaust system, a 4 into 2 into 1 with a vertical exit silencer hidden in the tail cover, was homologated for road use, fully complying with Euro3 emissions regulations. With this exhaust, the output was 180.8 horsepower at 13,750 rpm. Installing the 102 dB racing silencer and dedicated CPU unleashed the Desmosedici's full 200 horsepower.

The welded tubular steel trellis hybrid frame shared its geometry with the race bike. Just as on the racer, the street bike's rear subframe was high-temperature resin-type carbon fiber, and the extra-long swingarm was cast, forged, and pressed aluminum. The rear suspension geometry and layout were also identical to the GP6's, with the rear shock attached above the swingarm to a rocker hinged to the crankcase.

The suspension itself was straight off the GP6 and the most advanced available for a production motorcycle in 2007. This included a fully adjustable 43-millimeter upside-down Öhlins FG353 pressurized fork (PFF) with TiN-coated sliders. The rear shock was also Öhlins with rebound low-/high-speed compression and hydraulic preload adjustment. Also similar to the GP6 were the seven-spoke lightweight Marchesini forged and machined magnesium alloy 17- and 16-inch wheels. Special tires were developed in collaboration with Bridgestone (Battlax BT-01), the massive rear (200/55x16) shoehorned over the wide 6.25-inch rim.

As expected, the braking was also the highest specification available. The front radial Brembo brake calipers with 34-millimeter pistons were the first monoblock type to appear on a street bike. A radial master cylinder with a GP-style hinged lever and remote adjuster and a pair of semifloating 330-millimeter discs (the GP6 wet race setup) completed the front brake specification. Alan Jenkins created the carbon-fiber bodywork and color scheme. Jenkins was also responsible for the Desmosedici MotoGP aerodynamics. Two versions were available: the Rosso GP and the Team Version. A team sponsor decal kit was provided with each bike. Initial projections were for the production of 400 bikes a year, but ultimately 1,500 were produced for the 2008 model year. This was a motorcycle that brought a new meaning to the term "race-replica."

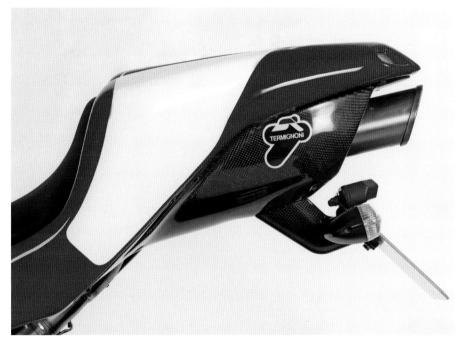

CHAPTER 24

1098 R BAYLISS LIMITED EDITION

2009 | 1,198cc liquid-cooled DOHC 90-degree twin | 106mm bore | 67.9mm stroke | 180hp at 9,750rpm | 364lb (165kg) | 186mph (300kmh)+

Considering the 999 won the World Superbike Championships in 2003, 2004, and 2006 and was still a highly competitive racer, its replacement for 2007 was something of a surprise. But while the 999 was extremely successful on the track, its style wasn't universally accepted, and it was still compared unfavorably to the 916 series. So for 2007 Ducati released the 1098, more powerful and lighter than the 999 and unashamedly drawing styling cues from the earlier 916.

Bayliss easily won the 2008 World Superbike Championship. In his final race, the 1098 was painted in special colors.

At the heart of the 1098 was an evolution of the Testastretta engine, with a 104-millimeter bore and 64.7-millimeter stroke, creating the first Ducati twin to displace more than 1,000cc. Weighing 11 pounds (5 kilograms) less than the 999 R, the 1098 was also more powerful, producing 160 horsepower at 9,750 rpm. The exhaust system now included a symmetrical 2-1-2 layout with Ducati's trademark twin under-seat silencers. The trellis frame featured a simplified tube layout of larger diameter, thinner-section main tubes, increasing rigidity and saving weight. But the most significant chassis update was a return to the 916-style single-sided swingarm. The fairing design marked a return to the 916's dual headlight arrangement instead of the 999's stacked type. Innovations initiated with the 1098 included Desmosedici-style digital instrumentation and electronic data acquisition. The overall package was superior to the 999.

The 2007 World Superbike regulations still limited twins to 1,000cc, thus making the 1098 ineligible. Consequently, Ducati continued to race the 999. For 2008 Ducati pressured the FIM to increase the capacity limit for twins to 1,200cc, threatening to quit the series if the rules were not changed. The FIM changed the rules, although twins were penalized 13 pounds (6 kilograms) compared to the 1,000cc fours. For the 2008 season, Ducati produced a 1,198cc version of the 1098. Troy Bayliss won 11 races to comfortably take his third World Superbike Championship. Bayliss won championships on three generations of Ducati Superbikes—the 996 R, 999 R, and 1098 R.

For 2009 the 1198 replaced the 1098. Following Bayliss' retirement from motorcycle racing, Ducati released the 1098 R Bayliss Limited Edition. As on the World Superbike racer, the Testastretta Evoluzione displaced 1,198cc through a longer bore and stroke over the 1098's. In the tradition of SPS- and R-series

Ducatis, the 1098 R was the most powerful production Ducati twin ever, producing 186 horsepower with the supplied race kit. To achieve this power safely, the 1098 R engine featured many specific components, including sand-cast crankcases, 34 percent lighter titanium connecting rods, molded carbon-fiber cam belt covers, and magnesium cam covers. The chrome nitride-plated titanium valves were larger (44.3 millimeters and 36.2 millimeters), and the high-compression 12.8:1 pistons featured the distinctive double rib under the crown developed for the MotoGP Desmosedici. This provided reduced friction and high strength with minimal piston wall surface area.

Many other features were inherited from the factory Superbike racer, including elliptical throttle bodies and twin injectors per cylinder. The 1098 R was the only street Ducati still with twin injectors. The first centrally mounted injector fed fuel through a four-hole nozzle while the second offset injector fed through a 12-hole nozzle. This ensured progressive and fluid power delivery throughout the rev range with the capacity to provide much more fuel under racing conditions. The six-speed transmission included a higher ratio sixth gear, and all the gears were of the same high-strength steel shot-peened for additional strength as in Ducati Corse race bikes. The 1098 R also featured a race-type slipper clutch and titanium and stainless-steel exhaust system.

The main frame was the same as that on the production 1198, but because the 1098 R was monoposto, the rear subframe was aluminum, allowing a 50-percent weight reduction in this area. The front 43-millimeter Öhlins fork and

The 1098's Testastretta Evoluzione engine was the first Ducati twin to displace more than 1,000cc.

monobloc Brembo brakes were unchanged from the production 1198 S, but the rear shock was a racing-style Öhlins TTXR. Other 1098 R features included the use of carbon fiber for the fairing belly pan, upper-fairing internal panels, tank lower side panels, seat assembly, and front fender. The 1098 R was also the first road bike to feature a racing-style traction control system.

The 1098 R Bayliss Limited Edition had a special color scheme designed by Aldo Drudi. Drudi was best known for Valentino Rossi's helmet designs, but he had created the Monster Foggy S4 in 2001 so had a design history with Ducati. Bayliss' World Superbike 1098 was painted in identical livery for his final race at Portimão in Portugal, and the paint design's important components were his trademark No. 21 and the Australian national flag contrasting with the white and red carbon-fiber bodywork. Other features specific to the 1098 R Bayliss were the matte black five-spoke wheels and carbon-fiber exhaust heat shield. Only 500 1098 R Bayliss Limited Editions were produced, and they were a fitting tribute to a great champion, the most successful Ducati rider after Carl Fogarty.

The 1098 wasn't as dominant in the World Superbike Championship after Bayliss retired. Veteran rider Noriyuki Haga managed a close second on the Xerox-sponsored 1098 in 2009; then Ducati withdrew from direct involvement. Its support passed to Carlos Checa and the satellite Althea Ducati team, and Checa rewarded Ducati with a dominating victory in the 2011 World Superbike Championship. Checa proved nearly unbeatable, winning 15 races on a machine deemed obsolete. As had happened in 2006 with the 999, the 1098 delivered a surprising result just as it was to be replaced, proving there was more life in the older design than anyone expected. Checa continued to race the earlier 1098 with moderate success, even after its replacement by the Panigale in 2012.

As the end of the Testastretta line for Superbikes, the 1098/1198 also represented the end of an era. These would be the last Superbikes with Pantah-derived engines and a tubular steel frame. The model may have only lasted five years, but the 1098's legacy will never be forgotten.

CHAPTER 25

DIAVEL

2013 | 1,198cc liquid-cooled DOHC 90-degree twin | 106mm bore | 67.9mm stroke | 162hp at 9,500rpm | 463lb (210kg) | 162mph (260kmh)

Entry into the American cruiser market had been a conundrum puzzling Ducati for four decades. It began back in 1963 when the then US distributor Berliner commissioned Ducati to design a Harley-style cruiser, the 1,260cc V-4 Apollo. Then, as now, Ducati specialized in sporting motorcycles, but Berliner wanted a slice of the lucrative police market dominated by Harley-Davidson. Ducati had Ing. Fabio Taglioni create the brilliant 90-degree V-4 Apollo concept bike. Decades ahead of its time, the 100-horsepower V-4 shredded its 16-inch Pirelli tires. Ultimately the project stalled. Fast forward to 1985 when Cagiva took over Ducati. Cagiva too wanted a slice of the US cruiser market. It rejected a bevel-drive 900cc cruiser, instead producing the Pantah-based Indiana between 1986 and 1990. This ill-conceived design was a failure from the outset and put the idea of a Ducati cruiser to rest for 20 years.

Ducati's exceptional racing results in World Superbike and MotoGP ensured it was well established as a premier sport bike manufacturer, but the US cruiser market was simply too large to ignore. In 2010, 48 percent of street bikes sold in the US were cruisers. Ducati, to the chagrin of many traditionalists, wanted its slice of that lucrative pie.

Ducati's answer was the Diavel (from the Italian *diavolo*, meaning devil and mutating to *diavel* in the Bolognese dialect), a radical new power cruiser providing surprising handling and performance. There was an established market demand for large-displacement, high-performance, cruiser-style motorcycles, such as the Yamaha V-Max and Harley-Davidson Night Rod, but the Diavel presented a radical version of this concept. It was a true hybrid: an essential light and agile naked motorcycle that could serve as either an imposing cruiser or a powerful sports bike. For the first time, all of these characteristics were incorporated in a single motorcycle.

The Diavel featured a Testastretta Evoluzione eight-valve engine derived from the Multistrada 1200. Valve overlap was reduced to 11 degrees (from 41 degrees on the Superbike) to smooth power delivery and improve fuel economy and emissions. The Diavel was also fitted with a heavier flywheel and a reduced compression ratio of 11.5:1 to improve bottom end and midrange response. Aesthetics play a crucial role for any cruiser, so the engine cases and timing belt covers were restyled. The cooling system played a role in the bike's look as well, its twin side-mounted radiators fed by large aluminum intakes. This cooling system design also allowed the engine to be moved forward, loading the front tire to improve grip and reduce wheelies under acceleration. Elliptical Mikuni throttle bodies with a single injector per cylinder, a distinctive 58-millimeter 2-1-2 catalytic exhaust with twin mufflers carrying lambda probe oxygen sensors, and a power valve all served to optimize power and torque delivery.

The 1,260cc Apollo was Ducati's first attempt at a US-style cruiser.

As on the Multistrada, the engine's versatility was expanded by an array of electronic rider aids, including eight-position Ducati Traction Control (DTC) and three riding modes. The Sport setting delivered the Diavel's full 162 horsepower and its sharpest response. The Touring setting offered the same power but with more progressive delivery. The Urban setting dropped output to 100 horsepower to ease in-town riding. But it was torque, not horsepower, that the Ducati design team concentrated on, as torque combined with lighter weight equals acceleration. And the Diavel engine was a torque monster, producing a stonking 94 lb-ft of torque at 8,000 rpm. The result was class-leading acceleration: zero to 60 miles per hour in a stunning 2.6 seconds. This was quicker than even the 1198 R Superbike.

The tubular steel frame followed traditional Ducati practice, with a new, long single-sided swingarm and a stout inverted Marzocchi 50-millimeter fork handling suspension duties. The fully adjustable Sachs rear shock absorber was mounted horizontally to allow a low seat height. Braking was to Superbike standards with twin Brembo 320-millimeter front brake discs and radial-mount Monobloc calipers. The rear disc brake, at 265 millimeters, was slightly larger than was typical for Ducati and was clamped by a twin-piston caliper.

The Diavel also featured new wheels with 14 triangular spokes. Ducati experimented with both 16- and 18-inch tire options, eventually settling on a massive 240/50x17 rear tire developed by Pirelli. This massive rear tire mimicked that used on the MotoGP GP10 Desmosedici and was designed to provide the correct visual aspect along with agility, neutral steering response, and high lean angles. It also required an equally massive 8-inch-wide rim.

Ducati's traditional creative approach in which engineering influences design was eschewed with style taking precedence. The styling was entrusted to Bartholomeus Janssen Groesbeek (better known as Bart), who had come to Ducati in 2002 after working for Yamaha's creative division, GK Design, which had designed the V-Max. US custom designer Roland Sands served as a consultant on the project. Bart provided the Diavel with muscular styling in keeping with the power cruiser theme, its visual aspect when viewed from the side suggesting a sprinter in the starting blocks. Many details imbued the Diavel with a strong identity, including a headlight with high- and low-beam double reflectors and a horizontal strip of LED running lights. An innovative number plate was mounted on the rear hub of the single-sided swingarm and employed a double strip of multifunctional LEDs for rear lighting. The Diavel was available in two versions: the Diavel and Diavel Carbon. The Carbon featured carbon-fiber bodywork, DLC-coated forks, a performance exhaust, and lighter forged and machined Marchesini wheels.

Unlike traditional cruisers, the Diavel was not strictly a straight-line package. This was a cruiser that could also handle turns. Despite its long 62.6-inch (1,590-millimeter) wheelbase, low seat height, and 28-degree steering rake, the Diavel could attain a maximum 41-degree lean angle. Creating a power cruiser unlike anything else was a difficult trick to pull off, but Ducati managed it and staked its claim to the American cruiser market.

CHAPTER 26

PANIGALE 1199 S TRICOLORE

2013 | 1,198cc liquid-cooled DOHC 90-degree twin | 112mm bore | 60.8mm stroke | 195hp at 10,750rpm | 362lb (164kg) | 186mph (300kmh)

Though the 1198 Testastretta was still a significant force in World Superbike, as evidenced by Carlos Checa's 2011 championship victory, by 2012 the Testastretta had reached the limit of Ducati's traditional evolutionary development. The basic engine architecture traced back 25 years to the 500cc Pantah, and many design features went back even further. The vertically split crankcases and ball main bearings, for example, harked back to the 1954 Marianna. It was time for Ducati to replace its traditional evolutionary process with one of revolution. The all-new Superquadro (oversquare) engine was the result. Only Fabio Taglioni's original 90-degree L-twin configuration and desmodromic valve control carried over from earlier designs.

1199 PANIGALE S

The Desmosedici RR inspired much of the engine design. The crankcases incorporated the cylinder outer water jacket with individual wet liners inserted into the crankcase apertures. This design enabled the cylinder heads to be secured directly to the crankcase, making a more rigid engine unit. Shell main bearings now supported the crankshaft, allowing more rigid, larger-diameter crank journals. Lubrication was uprated with a MotoGP-style vacuum oil pump that maintained constant vacuum in the crankcase underneath the pistons, controlling the internal crankcase pressure.

The 112x60.8-millimeter bore and stroke was the most oversquare of any production motorcycle engine and allowed for larger 46.8-millmeter and 38.2-millimeter valves. Ducati's traditional desmodromic system was ideal for the Superquadro's high rpm and large valves, the mechanical actuation allowing the rocker arms to follow cam lobes with steep profiles and radical valve timing. A ride-by-wire digital throttle, the first for a production Ducati Superbike, controlled twin injectors per cylinder in new Marelli 67.5-millimeter oval throttle bodies. Also for the first time on a Ducati Superbike was a wet, oil-bath slipper clutch featuring a self-servo mechanism that compressed the friction plates when under drive from the engine.

Perhaps the most radical new design feature was the replacement of the toothed belt-drive camshaft system first introduced with the Pantah in 1979. The long duration double overhead camshafts were now operated by a combined chain and gear-drive arrangement. A conventional chain ran from the crankshaft to the cylinder head where a single sprocket positioned between inlet and exhaust camshafts was attached, a gear meshing with gears on the ends of both camshafts. This was the first time Ducati had used a chain for the camshaft drive since the ill-fated parallel twin of 1975. An innovative decompression system allowed for a smaller battery and starter motor, despite

Carlos Checa led the official 2013 World Superbike Championship challenge on the Ducati Alstare Panigale.

the monster pistons. The Superquadro set a new standard for a twin, producing 195 horsepower, 25 more than the 1198.

Another significant departure from convention was the chassis, a die-cast hollow aluminum monocoque rather than the traditional tubular steel. This chassis was strongly influenced by the MotoGP Desmosedici carbon-fiber frameless type first introduced during 2009. The frame weighed just 2.2 pounds (4.3 kilograms) and doubled as an airbox containing the air filter and throttle bodies. The new design still used the engine as a stressed member, and the frame was responsible for half the 22-pound (10-kilogram) weight, saving over the 1198. The Superquadro engine was rotated backwards, with the front cylinder 21 degrees from horizontal, which enabled the engine to be positioned 32 millimeters further forward, improving front/rear weight distribution. A new fully die-cast aluminum single-sided swingarm was 1.5 inches (39 millimeters) longer than the 1198 and attached directly to the rear of the engine. This increased the wheelbase to 56.6 inches (1,437 millimeters) and contributed to the 52/48 percent weight distribution. With the engine basically serving as the frame, like the legendary Vincent twin, the entire package was extremely compact with its mass centralized.

Weight-saving measures extended to the exhaust system, which was relocated below the engine, allowing a lighter aluminum rear subframe. A magnesium front subframe supported the headlamp, instrumentation, and fairing. Suspension on the 1199 Panigale Tricolore was state-of-the-art, incorporating electronic riding mode technology with the Öhlins front and rear Ducati electronic suspension (DES) system. The 43-millimeter Öhlins fork was adjustable electronically for compression and rebound damping, while the Öhlins rear shock featured twin-tube (MotoGP and World Superbike)

technology offering separate adjustment for compression and rebound damping. This highly sophisticated system allowed suspension adjustment of preset or personal riding modes. Damping adjustment was achieved by signals to electronic actuators in the suspension units that executed the mechanical adjustment. Completing the 1199 Panigale Tricolore's awesome chassis package were 330-millimeter discs gripped by newly designed Brembo four-piston, dual pad, monobloc one-piece brake calipers and triple three-spoke forged aluminum Marchesini 17-inch wheels. The rear 200/55 tire was the widest ever fitted to a production Ducati superbike.

Another notable feature of the Panigale was the mind-boggling array of electronic aids. The ride-by-wire throttle (RbW) offered three ride modes: Race, Sport, and Rain. Other electronic systems included a sports Bosch ABS, traction control (DTC), electronic suspension (DES), quick shift (DQS), and engine brake (EBC). There was also electronic rear link ratio adjustment, providing ratios suitable for a passenger or solo riding. The dash featured a color thin-film transistor screen that automatically changed the background display depending on ambient light and selected riding mode. When stationary, the instrumentation could be used to personalize all electronic settings within each riding mode before saving. There was such a broad scope for fine tuning that serious riders needed a lot of time and plenty of experimentation to arrive at the right cocktail of settings to get the most out of the bike's enormous potential.

It was the most radical new design to ever emerge from Borgo Panigale, and the 1199 had a lot to live up to. It needed to look to the future while maintaining Ducati's traditional ethos. And the Panigale provided a brilliant solution: tradition maintained through the 90-degree engine layout with desmodromic valve actuation combined with a radical new approach to engine and chassis architecture.

PHOTO NOTES:
JAMES MANN

Shooting motorcycles in the studio involves a lot of careful lighting to make it look as though you haven't really done much at all. I was keen to ensure that as much of the bike as possible could be seen from each angle that I shot rather than trying be overly creative with highlights and shadow. We used a number of infinity-cove studios, in which the smooth, white floor and the wall merge with the ceiling in a seamless curve. We also built studios on location to photograph machines where no studio existed. In the full-cove studios, we used constant tungsten lighting bounced into the walls for focused highlights, as well as a small amount of direct lighting through a frosted screen to pick up detail in the profiles and three-quarter views. Location studios required a different approach, and we switched to direct flash through softboxes. No matter how good the images, there's always a lot of Photoshop work to do in tidying up points of focus and beefing up the saturation for the infinity cove images.

Camera
Canon EOS 5D Mk II

Lenses
17–40mm Canon f/4
50mm Canon f/2.8
70–200mm Canon f/2.8

ACKNOWLEDGMENTS

Many thanks to all the owners who generously lent their stunning Ducatis for this book–without them, it would not exist. Particular thanks to Scott Muir and his wife, Marjorie, and son, Jason, who put up with me staying in their home for the duration of shooting Scott's amazing collection and the chaos we created in his garage building the studio. Finally, to my wife, Sarah, who kept all in order at home as I buzzed all over the country shooting Ducatis.

James Mann

I would like to thank former Ducati design chief Pierre Terblanche for his insights over the years as well as his foreword for this book. Thanks as always to my family, Miriam, Ben, and Tim for their support.

Ian Falloon

INDEX